Techniques of Routing

Jim Phillips

E & FN SPON
An Imprint of Chapman & Hall

London · New York · Tokyo · Melbourne · Madras

UK   Chapman and Hall, 2–6 Boundary Row, London SE7 8HN

USA   Chapman and Hall, 29 West 35th Street,
New York NY 10001

JAPAN   Chapman and Hall Japan, Thomson Publishing Japan,
Hirakawacho Nemoto Building, 7F, 1-7-11 Hirakawa-cho,
Chiyoda-ku, Tokyo 102

AUSTRALIA Chapman and Hall Australia, Thomas Nelson Australia,
102 Dodds Street, South Melbourne, Victoria 3205

INDIA   Chapman and Hall India, R. Seshadri, 32 Second Main
Road, CIT East, Madras 600 035

First edition 1980
Second edition 1985
Reprinted 1986, 1991

© 1980 and 1985 International Thompson Publishing Ltd
and Jim Phillips
Typeset by Avon Communications Ltd, Nailsea, Bristol

Printed in Great Britain at the University Press, Cambridge

ISBN 0–419–15760–3

Contents

1. Introduction

Routology

The first British book on the subject of routing, published in 1980, was to be the first and the last! But, the interest in the router has grown astonishingly. As a mark of respect, it has been given an ...ology. The author would like to think he had something to do with it, as the term was not there in 1980, but no matter. Clearly, the router has become a fascinating machine both for the amateur and a most necessary one, for the commercial woodworker.

I have observed a growing band of users, who come between these two catagories – they are amateur and professional craftsmen, and include guitar makers, antique restorers, organ builders and clock-makers.

Let us review the progress and uses for the router.

Only a few decades ago, the hand router was to be seen only occasionally in the joinery shop: Its uses were mainly confined to making housings, rebates, tongues and grooves.

Quite a different story in 1984. The router has become a 'must' power tool, with the heavier duty ones being inverted and used legitimately as machine table routers. Clever attachments, and a vast array of cutting and shaping tools, are readily available. It now becomes a proposition for small joinery shops to purchase such equipment to carry out light machining as a back-up for the spindle moulder.

The advent of the 'plunge' router in the 1950's, better 'power to weight' ratio, and mass production, have all helped to bring prices down to acceptable levels. These factors have largely contributed to the growth of Routology. Routing devices, gadgets, jigs and template

THE ROUTING REVOLUTION

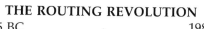

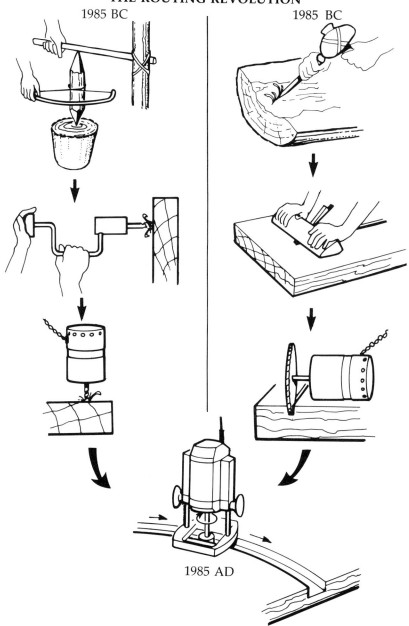

1985 BC   1985 BC

1985 AD

seem to generate unlimited possibilities. Routing is now practiced and 'dare say', enjoyed by almost everyone working wood. Handled correctly, the router will perform an even wider variety of jobs, as hopefully this book No. 2 will clearly show.

The drift towards traditional finishes provides a clue to the routers popularity. The current trend to abandon the 'plastic' appearance of modern day furniture, for example, is most noticeable. Classic shapes, ovolos, ogees and rounds, or combination of all these, are seen not just on cupboards, doors and tables, but on kitchen and bathroom fitments.

Summing up, one can say with confidence, routing technology is here to stay and further develop. It is a unique machine for fulfilling the whims of those with craft tendencies. It will surely play a fine role in encouraging constructive leisure time activities.

If this book has helped to achieve that end, it will have served a useful purpose, and given the author personal satisfaction.

Visual Symbol   Movements

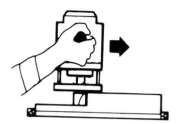

Router mobile.
Workpiece static.

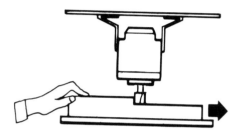

Overhead Router static.
Workpiece mobile.

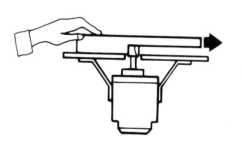

Inverted Router static.
Workpiece mobile.

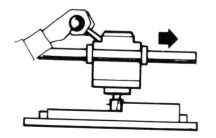

Mounted Router mobile.
Workpiece static.

CONCEPT 1995

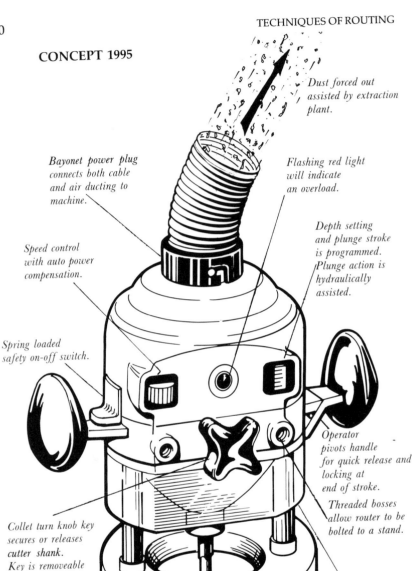

Dust forced out
assisted by extraction
plant.

Bayonet power plug
connects both cable
and air ducting to
machine.

Flashing red light
will indicate
an overload.

Depth setting
and plunge stroke
is programmed.
Plunge action is
hydraulically
assisted.

Speed control
with auto power
compensation.

Spring loaded
safety on-off switch.

Operator
pivots handle
for quick release and
locking at
end of stroke.

Threaded bosses
allow router to be
bolted to a stand.

Collet turn knob key
secures or releases
cutter shank.
Key is removeable
for use on either
side of motor.

Dust 'skirt' contains
the chips for extraction
vertically.

This book describes routers introduced in their thousands during the period 1960-1985. The technology for improvements has already arrived, and the design illustrated here, is not just a flight of imagination, but a prediction for 1995.

2.   Basic principles of the router

The router is now considered to be one of the most versatile machines used in the wood, plastics, and light-metal working trades. Few know who introduced the first router, since it evolved gradually from a rotary drill or cutter operated by hand. History illustrates man's resourcefulness in improving output, from a bow drilling device used as early as 10,000 B.C. (see Fig. 1.1) through to the achievement of the modern-day hand router. This book is designed to give the many tradesmen who own a hand router or intend to buy one, the benefit of practical experience and useful tips from trade users and craftsmen.

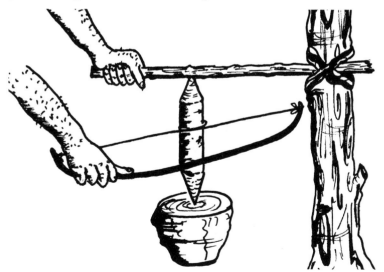

Fig.1.1. Even in 10,000 B.C., Stone Age man was striving and finding ways of using his hands more effectively.

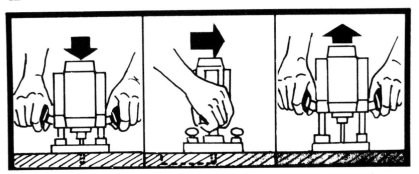

Fig.1.2. Basic principles of the plunging router, (Left to right) Plunge in and lock. Rout the groove. Release lock and spring up.

Many applications and suggestions may be 'old hat' to some tradesmen, but experience in the field has shown quite definitely that many firms have a thirst for knowledge about the capabilities of the hand router. Few firms offer satisfactory instruction manuals, even though the routing machine, if used to full advantage, will both increase production and drastically reduce labour costs.

The arrival of the 'plunging' type router in the 1940s caused a ripple of interest in the woodworking trade, but the then high cost of such routers with spring-loaded bases, prevented them from being generally accepted in the trade. Today, however, such routers as the Elu, with its ease of operation, and competitive price (close to that of a conventional hand router), are fast becoming standard equipment in the woodworking trades. Furthermore, with the price barrier removed, the more professional type of amateur is taking up routing as a constructive leisure occupation.

While we are praising the merits of the latest 'plunge' type routers, it should be stated here and now, that in no way are we depreciating the skill and fine work of craftsmen who have used the conventional router for over four decades. In skilled hands, these routers produce work equal to their modern counterparts.

There are numerous benefits in using a 'plunging' router, but the fundamental advantages are as follows:

Safety aspects

Factory inspectors are encouraging the use of routers with this plunging action, and the safety aspects almost speak for themselves.

When the 'plunging' router is used portably, the cutter only projects below the base when the operator is actually engaged in routing, i.e. when the router carriage is depressed, and the cutter is in the work. After each operation the carriage lock is released and the cutter retracts out of harm's way.

Simplicity

From experience, it has been found that semi-skilled labour with a modicum of commonsense, can use a 'plunging' router. The basic principle is shown in Fig. 1.2. With a few minutes teach-in, and a half hour or so practice, the elementary concept of setting up to do a job is mastered. The sequence of preparing the machine for work and actually operating it, becomes second nature very quickly.

Improved finish

The advantage of being able to position the base of the router firmly on the work-piece and to plunge the cutter down at 90 deg. is the all-important factor. It means a clean, square cut entry into the work and, similarly, when the routing job is completed, the retraction of the cutter at 90 deg. prevents any inclination to chip out the top surface. It is this confidence in being able to cut squarely that enables an operator to perform so quickly and yet accurately.

Good vision for working

The open type carriage of the 'plunging' router provides more room for changing the cutters, introduction of spanners, etc. Furthermore, when the 'plunging' router is depressed, the vision for sighting the work is excellent. It is important for the operator to see what he is doing at all times, when to start and when to stop.

Applications and router models

To describe the advantages and workings of the more progressive plunging router, we shall portray one such router generally accepted and used in the trade by woodworkers and craftsmen alike; this is the Elu MOF 96. It has a speed of 24,000 rpm, and is rated at 3/4 hp. It has a plunging depth of up to 2in. and weighs approximately 6lbs. There are a number of larger models in the range, which work on the same principle. The ones we shall be mentioning from time to time are the MOF 31 and 98, which have 1,200 and 1,600 Watt motors respectively. Heavy-duty applications in the woodworking trades require more powerful routers to perform the work satisfactorily, and these models can take wider and deeper cuts in one pass of the router.

During 1985 and 1986 most routers are being updated with variable speeds, better depth setting systems, and bases which will accept improved fences and attachments.

However, many thousands of routers have been produced since 1960 which are based on the designs described in this book.

Furthermore, other makes of routers from Europe, Japan and U.S.A. incorporating the plunge action, all operate on similar principles.

Setting up the router ready for work

The first step in setting up the router is to fix the cutter (see Fig. 1.4), but before fitting (or extracting) them always remove the electric plug from socket point. After ensuring that collet nut (9) is loose, the appropriate cutter is inserted into the collet (9A). Tightening the cutter involves holding motor spindle (9B) with 13mm open ended spanner and tightening the collet nut gently (no force) with 17mm spanner (both supplied with standard equipment). The standard collet supplied with this machine has a ¼in. (6.35mm) diameter opening to accept cutters with ¼in. diameter shanks. A wide range of cutters are available, and these are illustrated and described in the Appendix.

To set the required depth of cut, without switching on the motor, **depress the router on its spring loaded columns, (see Fig. 1.3) until the tip of the cutter rests on the workpiece: then lock the router in that position by turning the plunging knob (6) a quarter turn** clockwise.

Now adjust the depth of cut by sliding the depth bar (5) to the required position, and lock thumb screw (7). The distance between the base of the depth bar (5) and the screw head on the rotary turret stop (8) will be the depth to which the router will cut. Allow motor to spring back to original position by turning knob anti-clockwise. Router is now

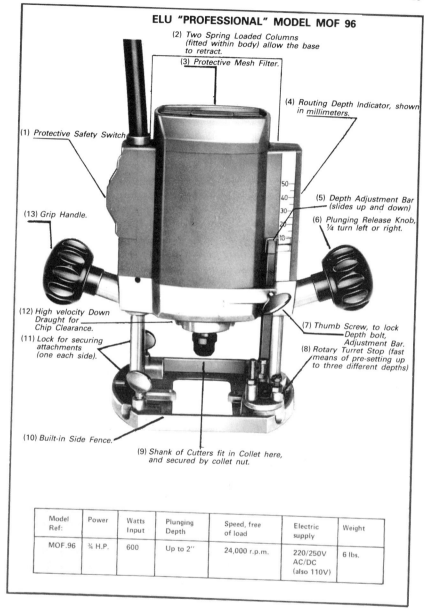

ELU "PROFESSIONAL" MODEL MOF 96

(2) Two Spring Loaded Columns (fitted within body) allow the base to retract.

(3) Protective Mesh Filter.

(4) Routing Depth Indicator, shown in millimeters.

(1) Protective Safety Switch

(13) Grip Handle.

(5) Depth Adjustment Bar (slides up and down)

(6) Plunging Release Knob, ¼ turn left or right.

(12) High velocity Down Draught for Chip Clearance.

(11) Lock for securing attachments (one each side).

(7) Thumb Screw, to lock Depth bolt, Adjustment Bar.

(8) Rotary Turret Stop (fast means of pre-setting up to three different depths)

(10) Built-in Side Fence.

(9) Shank of Cutters fit in Collet here, and secured by collet nut.

Model Ref:	Power	Watts Input	Plunging Depth	Speed, free of load	Electric supply	Weight
MOF.96	¾ H.P.	600	Up to 2"	24,000 r.p.m.	220/250V AC/DC (also 110V)	6 lbs.

Fig.1.3. This Elu Router is typical of the new 'plunger' type routers, its main features are described above.

ready to cut at the pre-set depth. Three alternative depths may be pre-set using the rotary turret stop.

To commence work

First switch on the motor (at switch (1)) and depress the router once more until the cutter has reached its full stroke, which has been pre-set by the depth stop. Without releasing hold on the handles, a quarter clockwise turn of the knob (6) will secure the motor in the depressed position. Routing can now commence, but note well, the router should be fed in the opposing direction to that in which the cutter is rotating (see Fig. 1.5).

When the routing operation is completed, the same knob (6) is given a quarter turn anti-clockwise, which allows the router head to spring up squarely from the workpiece. Work is now completed, and the motor should be switched off.

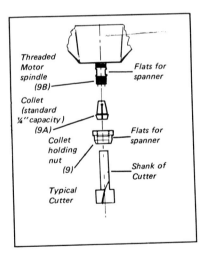

Threaded
Motor
spindle
(9B)

Collet
(standard
¼" capacity)
(9A)

Collet
holding
nut
(9)

Typical
Cutter

Flats for
spanner

Flats for
spanner

Shank of
Cutter

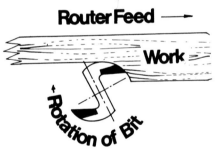

Fig.1.4. (Left) The cutter fixing system is clearly illustrated in the exploded view.

Fig.1.5. (Above) The router should be fed in the opposite direction to that which the cutter is rotating.

3. Main applications

Grooving

There is a misconception that router accessories are costly, indeed the most important device, namely the adjustable side fence, is normally part of the standard equipment, as with the Elu. Grooving, rebating, moulding and recessing can all be carried out using this one accessory. Grooving is one of the most popular applications for a hand router. No other method can produce a clean-cut and accurate slot so quickly. When making shelves, a routed groove ensures a good fit, especially if made slightly undersize.

For grooving narrow boards, a side fence (see Fig. 2.1) should be fitted to the machine to run against the long edge of the workpiece. For

Fig.2.1. The adjustable side fence slides into the router base.

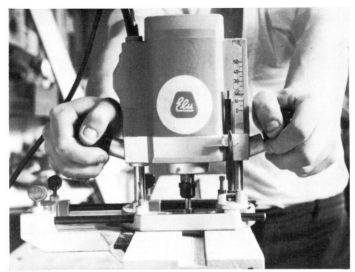

Fig.2.2. (Above) A drawer side needs a groove for the runner. The side fence, part of standard equipment, is used to advantage.

Fig.2.3. (Below) The router, with side fence fitted, was used to run a small groove along the edge of this casement window, for the insertion of weather stripping. Cutter Ref 3/4, 8mm ∅HSS was used.

Fig.2.4. The lateral fine adjuster offers a more delicate means of feeding in the side fence. It locates between the two rods on the fence and slots into a groove on the router base.

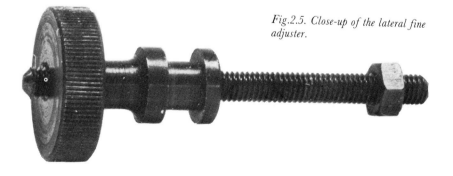

Fig.2.5. Close-up of the lateral fine adjuster.

Fig.2.6. The router is fitted with an extension, made from thin plastic. This ensures that the router continues on its parallel path, when leaving the workpiece. Note the 'overcut' board to support the side fence, which assists the process, and prevents chipping out when cutting across the grain.

example, a drawer side needs a groove for the runner (see Fig. 2.2) and a casement window needs a small groove for the insertion of weather stripping (Fig. 2.3). A useful accessory for adjusting the groove width, is a fine adjuster screw feed (see Figs. 2.4 and 2.5).

When using a side fence care should be taken to avoid cutting out of

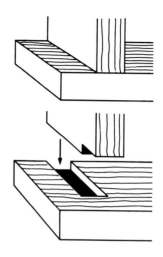

Fig.2.7. A shelf unit, strong and of pleasing
appearance, is a perfect way to show the value of the
router in furniture construction.

Close-up view of a stop groove which
gives a neat appearance to the joint.

true when finishing the run to the end of the board. A safety measure
which can be taken to guard against this is to fit an extension to the
inside of the side fence (using the two pairs of screws securing the
plastic liners). This can be made of thin plastic or plywood (see Fig.
2.6). An 'over-cut' board is also necessary. This serves two purposes; it
allows the side fence to continue along its parallel path, and at the same
time prevents the cutter chipping out as it leaves the workpiece and
enters the 'over-cut' board; this is most important when machining
across the grain.

When grooving on large flat surfaces, for example, a paired set of
bookshelf sides (see Fig. 2.7), the whole process is assisted if a
home-made grooving board (see Fig. 2.8) is used, since the housings
can be lined up squarely and clamped. It can be used, not only for

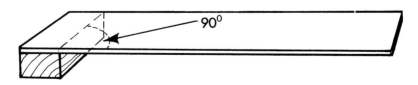

Fig.2.8. A grooving board greatly facilitates marking out and clamping.

Fig.2.9. A pair of stop groove housings being routed out from a single sheet.

Fig.2.11. (Below) Corners cut back.

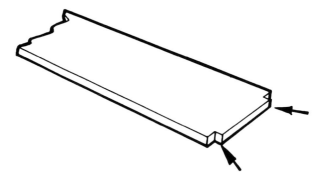

marking the positions of the housings out squarely, but also as a
runner or guide, along which the router will pass when grooving (see
Fig. 2.9). If the routed groove stops before the board edge is reached,
not only is a pleasing finish obtained, but also the shelf can be cut back
approximately $\frac{3}{8}$in. to allow for any shrinking in the shelf width (see
Figs. 2.10 and 2.11).

Fig.2.10. An exact matching pair of housings for a shelf unit. Note the routed grooves have stopped before the board edge is reached.

Extension Base

When light trimming or edging; it is a simple matter to retain the router firmly in the material. However, when a heavy routing cut is involved close to the edge of the board, there can be a tendency to tip over.

A baseplate is usually available to spread the surface area, but often this is inadequate.

Fig.3. With standard side fence, attractive geometrical patterns can be produced. In above illustration, a one flute router bit 3mm diam. Ref. 2/2 was used to obtain the fine grooved pattern. It is always advisable to extend the fence with a thin strip of plywood, to prevent run-off at the end of the pass.

An extended base with grip knob, can be of considerable help to avoid the possibility of tipping. Fig. 3.1 shows the router fitted with a home made sub-base extension.

Fig.3.1. A sub-base itted to the router will counteract the tendency to tilt over, when edging work is involved.

Direction of feed

For grooving across a board, the direction of feed is of no importance, but when edging, that is, rebating, trimming or moulding, there is a golden rule. Always ensure the feeding of the router is carried out in the opposite direction to that which the cutter is rotating. Cut in anti-clockwise direction for outside edging work. Cut in clockwise direction for inside work. See Fig. 3.2 and 3.4.

Avoid splitting out at corners

When edging a square workpiece in natural wood, as opposed to manmade board (e.g. chipboard, plywood, hardboard), there is a sequence for machining the edges to avoid split corners.

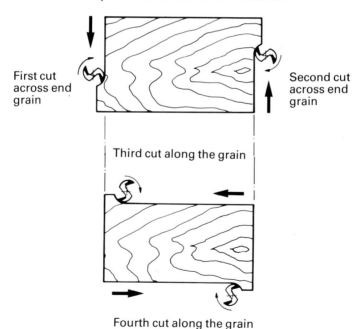

Outer profiling work – *cutting sequence.*
Always cut in anticlockwise direction.

First cut across end grain

Second cut across end grain

Third cut along the grain

Fourth cut along the grain

Fig.3.2.

One should first machine the sides running across the grain, followed by the sides, which run along the grain. See Fig. 3. Any breakouts shown at A and B, will be remedied when cutting with the grain.

If a shallow mould is to be undertaken, the above considerations are invalid, but for deep edging and actual cutting, adherence to the above is vitally important.

Alternatively, if extension pieces are clamped tight adjacent to the sides (along the grain), the splitting out problem can also be avoided. See Fig. 3.3.

Cutting sequence with extension pieces.

Top extension piece

With extension pieces clamped along the grain, chipping out at corners A & B is avoided. Always work anti-clockwise for outer profiling operation.

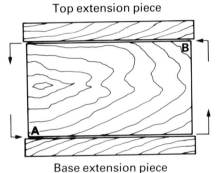

Base extension piece

Fig.3.3

Inner profiling work – *Always cut clockwise.*

When inside profiling work is involved, cut clockwise. (The opposite direction for outer profiling operations).

Fig.3.4.

Run-on/off boards

The finished edges of the workpiece may not be clean, if the question of 'break-out' has not been considered. Sometimes one can allow for this by making the workpiece oversize, and then trimming the edges off with a fine saw blade.

However, to avoid breakouts, when edging, rebating and grooving, there are various methods of overcoming the problem.

As can be seen in Fig. 3.2, direction of feed is important and sequence of operation, namely, cutting first across the grain so the 'with the grain' pass can 'clean' the breakout. However, sometimes, the grain is not square with the workpiece and a run-on/off board is a most useful introduction.

The one illustrated (Fig. 3.4), make by craftsman Bill Gates, is a little sophisticated, but worth making, to obtain best results.

The run-on/off board, shaded black, has one end adjustable, with clamps to ensure it butts up well against the stops. Note the simple eccentric clamp, which is designed to allow the router to take a path free from obstructions.

Rebating

Rebating for double glazing has great potential in the building and maintenance trades, particularly where house conversions and modernisations are concerned. If window frames are to be rebated after manufacture, or existing windows double glazed the procedure is as follows: first remove them and place them flat downwards on the workbench. An angular block is made (see Fig. 3.5) and fitted to the side fence in such a way that the cutter is proud of the corner, but no more than the depth of the rebate required. The router is guided round the internal edge of the frame, and by adjusting the depth of cut, the right amount of material can be removed to enable the second pane of glass, or complete double glazed unit, to be inserted. A wide cutter (ref. 4/2, see Chapter 17) to take the full rebate is recommended, with several passes to reach the required depth.

Lapping halving and jointing (see Figs. 3.6 and 3.7) is an excellent example of a time-saving application for the router. Battens are grooved and rebated at predetermined positions for the production of the framework. The battens are lined up accurately and clamped

Fig.3.4. This home-made grooving jig is adjustable, so that run-on boards can butt up against the board edges to avoid splitting out at the corners. Note the sliding wing nut clamp and eccentric clamp to apply pressure against run-on stop board.

Fig.3.5. Rebating a window to accept a second glazing panel, is shown being done with the Elu router.

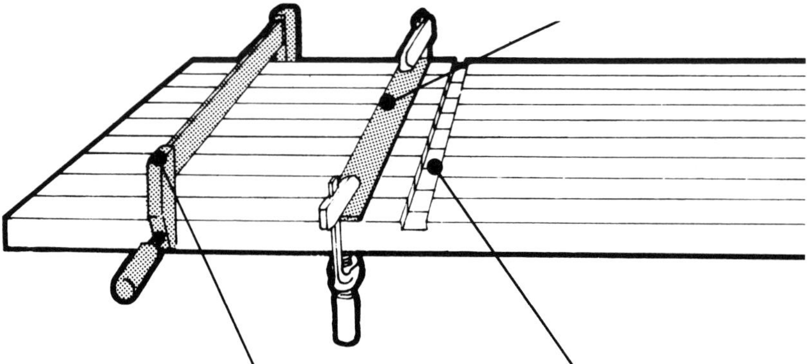

Straight edge clamped to battens

Clamp 'Side Stacked battens'   **Battens cross halved in batches**

Fig.3.6. (Above) Here is an accurate and fast way of cross halving and tee halving joint with a router. The battens are side stacked and clamped.

Some typical joints which can be made with the Router.

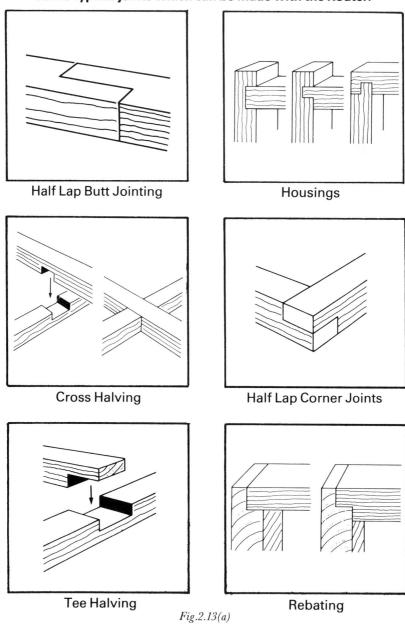

Half Lap Butt Jointing   Housings

Cross Halving   Half Lap Corner Joints

Tee Halving   Rebating

Fig.2.13(a)

Fig.3.7. (Left) Battening will all be identically cut, if clamping has been carefully carried out previously, and router passed squarely across the material.

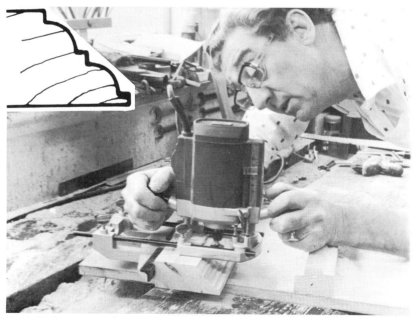

Fig.4. Multi-mould effects obtained by varying the depth of cut; full use being made of the wide variety of mould cutters now available (see Appendix).

together on one edge, then the 'plunge depth' of the router is set to half that of the batten. Using a clamped on straight edge, the router is then passed across the battens to the required depth and width.

Ideally, a cutter whose width is equal to the batten width should be chosen, so as to limit the number of passes. However, the number of passes needed depends also on the power factor of the router. When using 1½in. by ¾in. battening, for example, a 3/4 hp router would need six passes, a 1½ hp router four passes, and a 2 hp router two passes. Naturally, this is for approximate guidance only, but emphasis should be on making a clean cut without overloading the motor. The tone of the motor will indicate whether or not you are doing this.

Other machining operations

It is not generally realised that multi-mould effects can be achieved by taking a number of passes at different depths and widths, resulting in a very attractive finish. The temptation to take too much material off in one pass must be resisted. The mould shown in Fig. 4, was obtained by taking up to six passes, with the outer edge being machined before the inner part. Maximum advantage was taken of the rotary depth stop to reach a new depth in seconds; this most attractive feature of the 'plunge' router is discussed in Chapter 2.

By selecting the right cutter shape and size, a number of additional grooving and rebating operations may be undertaken. To name two:

Rebate and 'bird's beak' joints for joining acrylic sheet (Fig. 5);

Drop-leaf table made using two separate cutters (see Fig. 6).

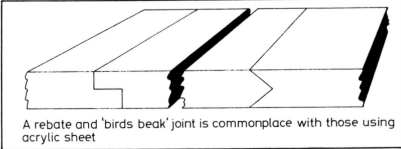

A rebate and 'birds beak' joint is commonplace with those using acrylic sheet

Fig.5.

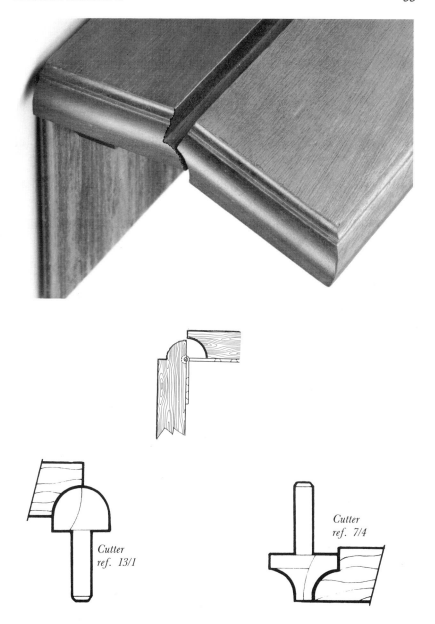

Fig.6. A drop-leaf table is created by using concave and convex cutters to ensure an exact fit. Cutters are shown in Chapter 17.

Panelling

While moulded sections can be 'planted' on flat surfaces, 'panelling' here refers to work where the router is applied direct to the board face. Man-made boards do not lend themselves to this application unless the workpiece is to be painted, but natural timber, especially hardwood, can be most attractively panelled out with the careful use of cutters now available. (Cutters suitable for this purpose are illustrated in Chapter 17.

Fig.6.1. A typical example of panelling work using an ovolo cutter. The plunging router with its 90 deg. entry is invaluable for the central mould work.

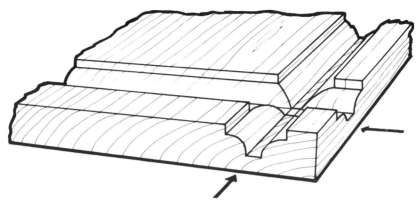

Fig.6.2. This clearly shows the attractive effects of straight parallel cuts using radiused cutters in conjunction with a straight edge.

For internal moulds (see Fig. 6.1), when no lead-in from the side is possible, the 'plunge' router is invaluable. It ensures a 90 deg. entry and a continuity in the moulded edges without imperfections. The same cutter is used to profile an ovolo mould, with only the side of the cutter engaging on the board edge. The router used in Fig. 6.1 was a heavy duty model Elu MOF 98, rated at 1,600 Watts; with this model, the panelling cut was grooved out in one pass. This is preferable to making several passes with a smaller, lower rated machine. It does not mean, however, that a 3/4 hp router, for example, could not be used for this purpose, but extra care would be required. The temptation is to take too heavy a 'bite', which would overload the motor and reduce the number of revolutions, resulting inevitably in a poor finish.

Parallel cuts can be made with the side fence of the router if the moulded panel cuts are reasonably close to the edge, otherwise straight edges or a template sheet can be used. When the mould runs off the edge on the cross grain (see Fig. 6.2) an over-cut board is essential to avoid the grain splitting out. Always use a fence extension as well, to maintain the router on an even path.

A multi-panelled door provides an excellent opportunity to produce attractive and unusual effects. The influx of cheap imported doors from the Far East should be a stimulus for original thinking for designs in moulded panelling work. The latest range of mould cutters shown in the Appendix offers such possibilities. One idea for a front door is to introduce small panel inserts, each insert having a criss-cross panel shape to provide a unique effect (see Fig. 6.6).

Fig.6.4. A fine example of corner moulding where a number of passes have been made with three different cutters. See Fig. 0.00.

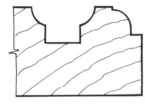

Fig.6.5. Cross section of wood showing clearer the mould shapes, produced by three passes of the router.

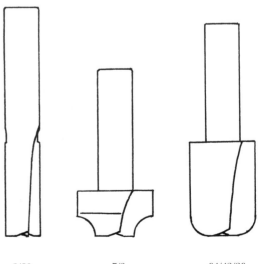

Cutter Refs.	3/50	7/2	84/42/38
	square groove	outer mould	double cove

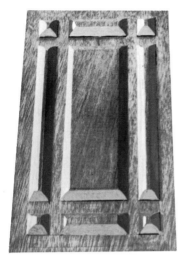

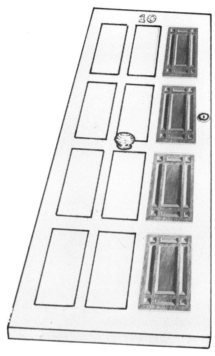

Fig.6.6. Example of attractive panelling on a front door. Straight routing cuts are used with radiused grooving cutters of various dimensions. A straight edged batten is used instead of the side fence.

Avoiding burn marks

The reasons for burn marks are either that the cutter is blunt, in which case the finish will be poor also, or more often the feed speed is too slow.

However, the argument that sometimes one must feed slowly, because the job demands it, is quite valid e.g. intricate shapes which have to be carefully negotiated. Furthermore, when entering the router from above, as when relief carving, panelling or stop grooving, the cutter may burn at the bottom of the groove at point of entry.

Fig.6.8. Routed groove free of burn marks.

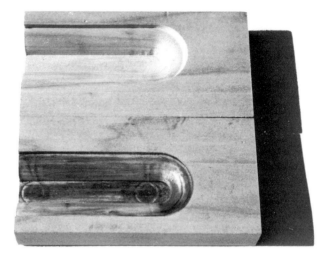

Fig.6.7. Burn marks due to slow feed speed.

The reason for burning, is the inability of the chips to clear in time before heat from friction can escape, but some wood is more inclined to burn than others (Fig. 6.7).

There is a way out of this problem which is basically simple. If you are grooving say to a 12mm depth, set your router for a 10mm plunge on your turret stop guage. Then take a second pass to remove the last 2mm. This will remove the burn marks left by the 10mm pass (Fig. 6.8). If initial marks still present a problem, start your work in the centre of a run, rather than at either end, and work backwards.

Refer to Chapter 15 for information on feed speeds, care and maintenance of cutters etc.

Concealed ducting

Electric cables and telephone wires, often need to cross doorways, and rooms at floor level.

A recessing system is available so as to hide and protect such cable. The procedure is as follows: A 3″ wide hardwood panel, suitably radiused on one side, is given a saw cut along its length. A keyed circular slot is now made along the saw cut using a router fitted with a key slot cutter. See Figs. 7 and 7.1 which describe this procedure visually.

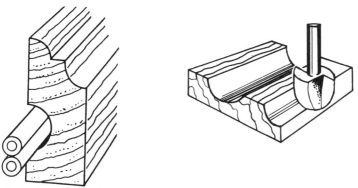

Fig.7. Skirtings can be recessed and radiused with Ref. 12 or 13 group of radius cutters.

Slotted hardwood board is recessed to accept floor cables, wires, etc.

Key slot cutter
with narrow neck
Ref. 84/37/14

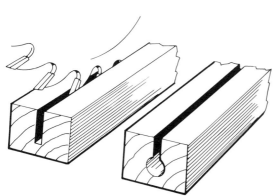

Fig.7.1. The slotting operation must be preceded with a saw to accommodate the narrow neck of the cutter.

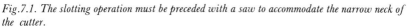

Using up scrap timber

Obtaining wide boards is a very expensive exercise in countries such as the U.K. where such material is imported. Narrow offcuts, and packing case wood are easier to come by, and often seasoned and free of knots. If edges are planed square they can be glued and butt jointed. However, a new type of joining system giving a longer glue line, is introduced in the form of a radiused tongue and groover. The circular plaque illustrated in Fig. 8.2, was made up from seven sections of wood – a mixture of oak, elm and mahogany offcuts, also Brazilian packing case battens. Matching tongue and groove joints were formed on their edges, using ref. 8 and 9 cutters, illustrated at Fig. 8. When glued and clamped, immensely strong joints were formed.

Another interesting application for these matching cutters, is in the forming of hinged joints, similar to a drop leaf joint, but with a draught proofing feature. See Fig. 8.1.

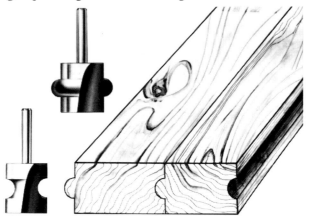

Fig.8. The glue line is elongated when the 8 and 9 group of T and G radiused cutters are applied for joining operations.

Fig.8.1. For dust-proof hinges, these radiused tongue and groove cutters are invaluable.

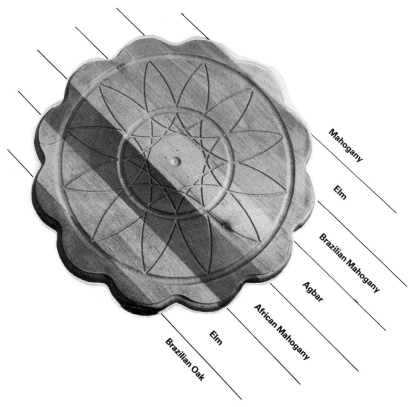

Mahogany

Elm

Brazilian Mahogany

Agbar

African Mahogany

Elm

Brazilian Oak

Fig.8.2. Scrap timer and offcuts are used to good effect by jointing and shaping into this attractive plaque. Jointing was performed with radiused jointing cutters refs. 8/10 and 9/11. Edge shapes were made utilising a trammel system.

'Ski' attachments

If crossbars are fitted to the router base, a means is provided for deep or shallow recessing, when a flat even surface is required below the level of the work surface. This device has been found invaluable for groundings in relief carving. It works like this. A pair of identical flat narrow sections of timber are clamped astride the workpiece. The router supported by the 'Ski', is plunged to remove 1 and 2 mm depth of material. The router is passed backwards and forwards, so as to skim across the work surface, ensuring that a smooth surface is

Above. The router is seen removing the groundings for a relief carving operation.

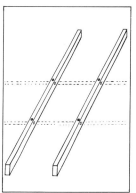

Left. A sketch showing the 'Ski' recommended, which acts as a sliding frame to hold the router parallel, but out of contact with the actual workpiece. This 'Ski' was made from 1" × ¼" m. steel.

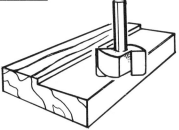

Fig.9. Special three winged surfacing cutter (Ref. 37/1) is especially suitable for obtaining a flat smooth surface.

obtained. Note that the router base does not come into contact with the workpiece. If the router is fitted with a 3 wing surface cutter Ref. 37/1, (or a large 2 wing cutter in this 4 group) a clear smooth bottom cut can be obtained. (See Fig.9.)

Boxing-in pipework

Even pipes can be attractively encased with a little imagination. If a decorative bead is cut on the edges of the box structure, the encasement can blend in with the furniture. The area within the box can be filled with polystyrene beads to retain the heat. A further bonus for the project.

The top surface can be utilised for displaying decorative plate, silverware, ect.

The cutter used for this finish was a Ref. 19/20, which has a $\frac{5}{16}''$ radius. (See Fig. 10.)

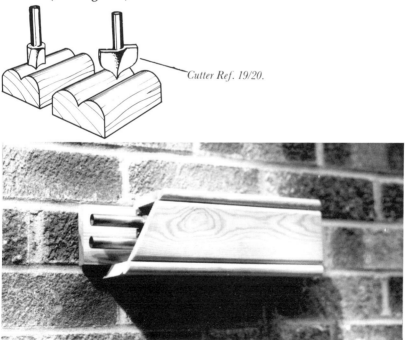

Cutter Ref. 19/20.

Fig.10. Boxed-in pipework can be given an attractive appearance if a decorative bead is applied to the corner edges.

4. Freehand and circular work

Freehand patterns and shapes can be cut expertly in the surface of thick material with surprisingly little practice. Freehand work can best be described as using the router without a guide fence, guide bush or other aids. The design is first marked out on the surface, preferably with a felt pen. The router is placed in position, the motor is switched on and the cutter is plunged into the workpiece to a pre-determined depth (use the adjustable depth bar). This technique of freehand cutting in practised hands, is clearly shown by the cut-outs made on soft insulation board to recess steel RSJ's, and pipework (see Fig. 11). If thin material is involved, one can cut right through and use the router as a 'Jigsaw' (see Fig. 11.1).

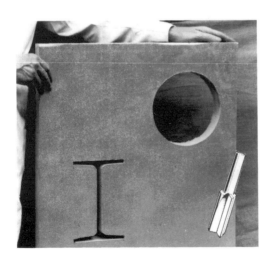

Fig.11. A typical application of deep freehand work by a firm of insulation contractors. A heavier duty router, namely the model Elu MOF 31, was used to plunge through the 2 in. thick material. A hand jigsaw would have 'run out' at the bottom edge, due to the thickness.

Cutters in the 4 group range can be supplied with 50mm length of cut. These cutters, used with the Elu router which has deep plunging facilities, provide the right combination to solve the problem.

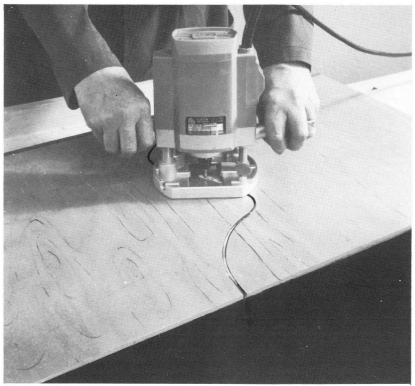

Fig.11.1. The router being used as a 'jigsaw'. With a little practice, one can become quite an expert in following a marked form. With a light duty router, however, one should limit the thickness of the board to 6mm, so as to avoid cutter breakage.

Fig.11.2. Routing 'house names' in a rough sawn oak panel.

Examples of freehand grooving work

A typical freehand grooving operation, which is often done with a router, is the cutting of house names into plaques (see Fig.11.2). More often than not, such work in commercial circles is done with a template, when a guide bush is fitted. Template routing is a subject which deserves full attention, and Chapter 5 is devoted to it.

Another illustration of freehand work (Fig. 11.3) shows the hand router being used to create a 'how to get there' message. Freehand

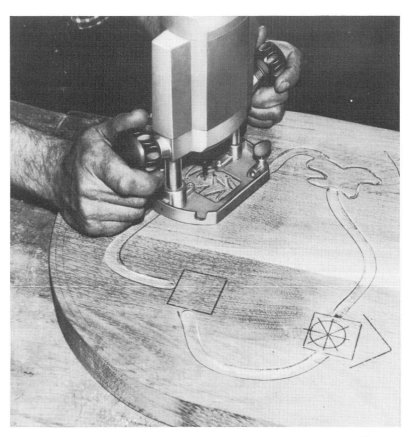

Fig.11.3. An illustration of freehand work. The hand router is being used to create a 'how to get there' message. Freehand engraving in solid hardwood can be a most absorbing pastime, and in skilled hands, most effective.

engraving in solid hardwood can be a most absorbing pastime, and in skilled hands, most effective.

Chair leg moulding

A simple means is provided for cutting a corner mould (2mm or 3mm rad) on to a chair or small table leg.

A self-guide 'beading' cutter forms part of the radius, and by turning the workpiece over and cutting from the opposite end, the second cut completes the shape. Fig. 11.4 portrays the procedure clearly.

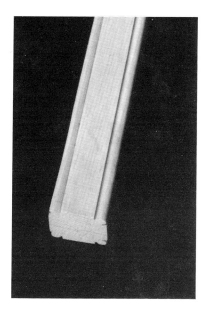

Corner mould cuts have been made on the four corners of this chair leg.

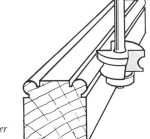

Fig.11.4. Corner Bead Cutter with self-guide roller bearing.

The fine depth adjuster

Sometimes, for such work as engraving, fine adjustment is needed. For this purpose, a fine depth adjuster (see Figs. 11.5 and 11.6) is fitted in place of the depth adjustment bar. This fixed to studding on the turret depth stop.

Edging work

Freehand bevelling, moulding and rebating can be carried out, even on shaped edges, by using cutters with guide pins mounted on their bases (see Fig. 11.7). The procedure for using these cutters is to set the depth so that when the guide pin is resting against the edge of the board, the

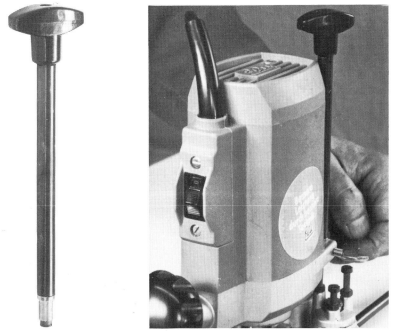

Fig.11.5. (Left) The fine adjuster above can be fitted in place of depth adjustment bar. This provides a slow feed for such work as engraving.

Fig.11.6. (Right) The fine depth adjuster (Fig.11.5.) is rotated clockwise and anti-clockwise to bring the cutter up and down approximately 1 mm per full turn.

cutter engages on the top corner edge of the board. To sum up, the guide pin of the cutter acts as the guide, and, if care is used, a well formed bevel or mould can be produced on the edge in a remarkably short space of time. Practice runs on scrap wood are recommended, so as to learn the technique. If too much pressure is exerted the guide pin will score or burn the edge of the workpiece. In the sign-making trade, these cutters are used extensively for bevelling acrylic, and operators have developed great expertise.

Often it is found to be more convenient to manipulate the workpiece against the cutter. For this purpose, the router is inverted with the cutter protruding through the table top. A special profiling table can be bought for this purpose, although a home-made one can be fabricated. Routing tables, or light 'spindles' as they are known in the trade, provide for a number of useful machining possibilities. These will be described in Chapter 12.

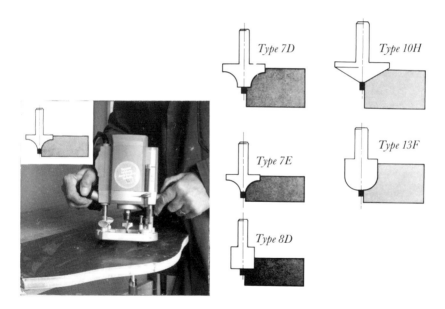

Fig.11.7. (Left) Freehand edge moulding using a radius cutter with guide pin follower.

Fig.11.8. (Right) Some popular free-hand self-guide cutters. These have guide pins in their bases, which follow the edges of the underlying material.

'Free-hand' edging

The professional approach to edge moulding operations can be broadly divided into two. For straight edge moulds or chamfers the usual practice is to use a side fence, but for shaped workpieces such as the shield illustrated at Fig.11.9, a self-guide bearing cutter comes into its own.

The project involves the production of a pair of Trophy Shields from 1¼" thick mahogany (see Fig. 11.11).

The shields are first bandsawed out rough and then shaped by hand, or with router and template. The 35 deg. bevel on the edges is cut with the router using a Ref. 46/35 TC Cutter, see Fig.11.10. The router is applied in an anti-clockwise direction, with the roller bearing guide engaging on the lower edge, and the cutter implanting the chamfer on the upper part.

Anti-tip support

When the router is used for edge trimming operations, the workpiece usually needs some support around the working area, to prevent the router from tipping.

Fig.11.9. (Left) The router is seen putting a chamfer on the perimeter. Direction of cut was anti-clockwise. The novel anti-tipping block, ensured the router was parallel at all times.

Fig.11.10. (Right) Cutter used for this operation was a ref. 46/35 giving a 35° chamfer cut. The roller bearing follows the contour of the workpiece.

Fig.11.11. A typical shield produced on the lines recommended.

A useful anti-tipping device can be made, consisting of a block of wood attached to the router guide rods, the same thickness as the workpiece. It is fitted so that the router base is level at all times with work surface (see Fig. 11.9).

Circular work

The trammel bar, or scribing arm as it is sometimes called offers numerous possibilities for decorative flat and inlay work. Shaped articles can be cut out, and attractive mould features produced. A fine example of this is shown in Figs. 14.9 and 14.8, where a grandfather clock face is under construction. Most attractive geometric shapes and curves can be made with a little imagination.

When engraving work only is involved, the depth stop is adjusted to give a shallow cut, but if extra fine adjustment is needed, the depth bar is replaced by a fine adjusting rod. If rotated clockwise or anti-clockwise, it lowers the cutter slowly in and out of the work. (It locates into the turret depth-stop head.) If deep grooving is involved, the procedure is to set the turret stop to cut in stages. Each completed circle would require the turret stop to be rotated to allow the router to cut to a greater depth. Carried one stage further, this system can be used to cut right through the material (see Fig. 12.8). Articles such as round table tops and wooden tableware can be cut without using a template (see Fig. 12.9). Edges can be moulded by merely substituting the grooving cutter with a moulding cutter, but the same centre point must be retained.

A useful tip to avoid marking the surface of the workpiece with the centre point of the trammel bar, is to fix a thin piece of plywood on to the work surface (see Fig. 12.10). It can be secured with double-sided adhesive tape. In this way the fulcrum point of the bar is pressed into the plywood rather than the work surface. When the work has been completed, the plywood is removed.

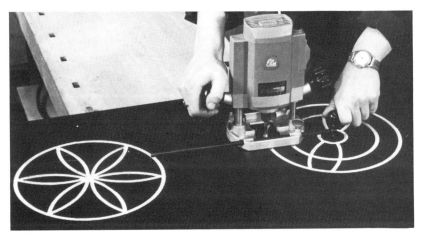

Fig.12.3. Attractive geometrical shapes for an inlay can be engraved when a beam trammel is used for the radius work.

Fig.12.4. (Below) Circular patterns cut into wood and acrylic show the unlimited possibilities open to those with artistic trends.

Fig.12.5. A home-made compass is invaluable for experimenting and marking out the fulcrum points, prior to cutting.

Fig.12.6. A decorative wall panel being made from high density blockboard. One flute, radius and ovolo cutters were used. See Appendix.

Fig.12.7. Examples of attractive engraving work using the beam trammel and the router.

Fig.12.8. (Above) by adjusting the depth of the router in stages, the beam trammel can be used to cut out a table top, bread board, or just an attractive wall plaque.

Fig.12.9. (Left) Table tops can be cut, moulded and trimmed if the same fulcrum point is used throughout.

Edging table tops

Attractive moulds and reed edge patterns can be cut in several ways.
The table top can be first rough cut with band saw or jigsaw, and
then profile cut from a beam trammel mounted on the router.
The two flute router bit is now replaced with a mouldiing cutter.

*Fig.12.10. A protective sheet of polywood is fitted to table top with double sided tape. This protects
the table top being marked with the fulcrum point of the beam trammel.*

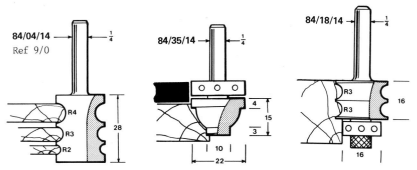

*Fig.13. Three typical edging cutters. The 84/35/14 has been fitted with a self-guide bearing on
the shank so as to follow a top mounted template.. The 84/18/14TC reeding cutter has a
self-guiding bearing mounted on its base so as to run along the lower edge of the material.*

Both the cutting and shaping can be attempted by using the one moulding cutter. Several passes will be needed due to the excessive stock removal. If it is a reeded shape, profile first with a narrow straight cutter (several passes to avoid breakage), then apply your reeded cutter which should be a self guided variety. E.g. refer 84/18/14 Fig. 13.

If your choice of reed is one which leaves no space for the roller to run along, then a Template should be cut simultaneously with the original profile cutting operation.

Some routers have edge following devices, which allows normal cutters to be used.

Cutting small radii

There is a limitation to the reach of a standard beam trammel since the router base restricts the radius to approx 3 in. However, there are several ways of overcoming this problem.

a) If a 'false' base is stuck (double sided tape) to the router base, a reversed screw point can provide the fulcrum point. However, adjusting the screw position each time to change the radius, can be tiresome.

b) The author made an adjustable beam trammel which was built into the false base (illustrated at Fig. 13.4). The fine fence adjuster was devised to bring the fulcrum point to the required position. The tongue was dovetailed to slide in and out of the 'false' base. Material was Darvic plastic, subsequently changed to Tufnol, because of instability.

c) Should it be acceptable for a hole 6mm diam. to be made in the centre of the workpiece (a cover plug could be introduced to hide it), then a pin or fibre dowel can be used as a fulcrum point. This is driven in to the centre hole, with 4mm projecting upwards. A 'false' base fitted to the router should have a series of 6mm holes drilled, which will locate in the projecting fulcrum pin. By 'spinning' the router at different location points, small circular patterns can be obtained.

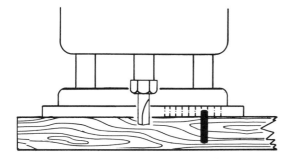

Fig.13.1. 'False' base with drilled holes, locate onto projecting pin driven into workpiece. The interchange of location points vary the radii of the 'trammel'.

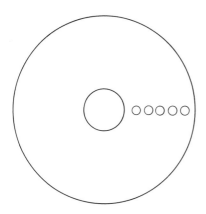

Fig.13.2. 'False' base drilled holes represent the location points into which the 6mm pin fixed in the workpiece, will fit. Centre hole should be at least 30mm diam. for chip clearance.

Fulcrum peg

With the feasability of cutting and routing small and large radii, new avenues for innovation are opened up.

If the fulcrum point is replaced by a peg, consisting of a pin or metal bolt, approx. 4mm or 6mm in diameter, a more secure fulcrum is obtained. See Fig. 13.2.

As will be seen in illustration 12.7 attractive shapes can also be cut from the surplus area of the workpiece.

The edges of the final workpiece can be further machined on a router table using a self-guide profile cutter. See Fig. 13.

Alternatively this system for cutting radii, can be applied to the

Fig.13.4. For small radii, under four inches, the stnadard beam trammel is oversize. This home-made mini-trammel, overcame this problem. The fine adjuster was fitted to a slide on the router base to bring the fulcrum in and out.

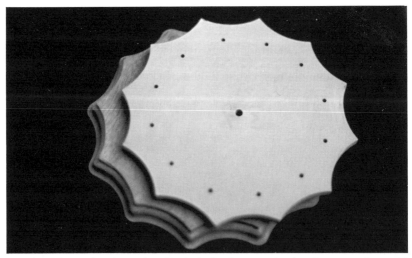

Fig.13.5. The template shown above has dual roles. Its conventional use is a pattern for a guide bush followers, and its second use is for producing a series of convex rotary cuts. The fulcrum point on the trammel is replaced by a pin or bolt which locates in the pre-drilled holes.

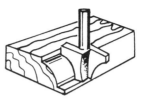

Type 7/4

Fig.13.6. Proposed candle-stick base. Three identical mahogany discs were cut using a mini-trammel, with two moulds introduced, first ovolo Type 7/4, then radius cutter, type 13/1 on the top edge. It shows how the router can be used for work normally only undertaken with a lathe.

Type 13/1

Fig.13.7. Having marked out 12 fulcrum points with compass, half circle cuts are made using the mini beam trammel described. If the material is above ¼″ thick, a series of 'sweeps' are needed, letting the cutter down by rotating the vertical fine adjuster on the router, in a clockwise direction. The central cut out part was used as a template to produce the bread board shown in Fig. 13.5. In Fig. 13.8, the same part is being edge moulded.

A typical ogee self-guiding cutter fitted with a ½" Ø roller bearing ref. 46/24.

Fig.13.8. The above illustration shows how the central part of the workpiece can be removed and the edge moulded by engaging the workpiece on a fixed cutter head. For this purpose the router has been inverted to form a machine router table. In operation the edges are shaped by rotating the workpiece against a self-guiding cutter which has a bearing mounted on its base.

Fig.13.9. From the template 'star' pattern (see Fig. 13.5) a bread board was cut and shaped in a most attractive way. The odd stripes in the board denote the different narrow timbers which were jointed together using cutters, ref. 8 and 9. See Fig. 13.10.

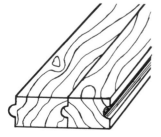

Fig.13.10. Narrow strips were jointed using convex and concave cutters Ref. 8 and 9.

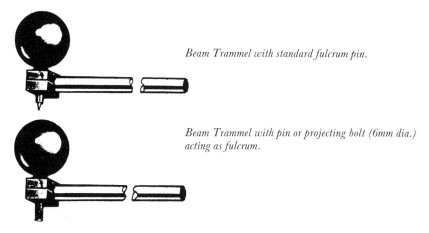

Beam Trammel with standard fulcrum pin.

Beam Trammel with pin or projecting bolt (6mm dia.) acting as fulcrum.

making of templates, which can be used many times over. The same fulcrum points are used for varying radii, and by interchanging cutter styles, making passes through the work at differnt depths, the possibilities are fascinating and unlimited in scope.

For clarification, the author has used melamine faced chipboard, in the illustrations, but when the system is applied to natural timber, most attractive work can be produced.

Fig.14. A precision home built beam trammel produced for circular cutting and shaping a grandfather clock face.

Beam trammel project-clock face

A fine example of circular cutting and shaping is produced by Mr. Ralph Fellows, Master Craftsman, and winner of numerous prizes for his superb woodworking achievements.

Not satisfied with the standard trammel, he produced his own precision like one, illustrated at Fig. 14.

This has fine adjustments on it, most necesary to cope with the numerous radii involved with its clock head face, and door. See Fig. 14.8.

He also produced a sliding clamp arrangement for adjusting the material and holding the material finely, in such a way that no obstruction hindered the routing operations. See Fig. 14.1.

Procedure for cutting and shaping

The sequence for machining can best be described by illustrations and sketches. Refer Fig. 14.2–14.7.

Fig.14.1. A sliding clamp arrangement to secure the workpiece, without resorting to clamps which would obstruct operations.

Fig.14.5. This illustration shows the top rail which has been cut with a ref. S3/22 long reach two flute cutter.

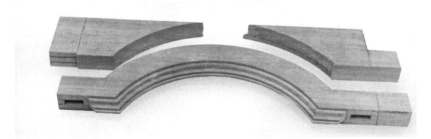

Fig.14.6. This illustration shows the top rail with finished mould and already morticed to accept the stiles. Refer to Fig. 14.2 which shows the sequence of operations for beam trammel work in this project.

Fig.14.7. Initial cut is made with a long reach solid TC cutter Ref. S3/22.

Fig.14.2. Procedure for shaping top rail of a clock face.

With shaped cutter fitted, the router is applied to edge mould the base of the rail. Note the support board butting up against lower edge. This prevents the router from tipping.

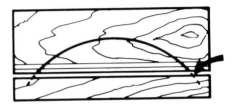

Straight, long reach narrow cutter is now fitted in place of the shaped one. Beam trammel is now mounted and set at 90 deg. to workpiece. With a series of sweeps from left to right. Shaded portion is cut away, leaving a square ege. The support board should butt up against the workpiece to prevent chipping out – see arrow.

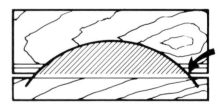

Using the same radius, substitute the straight cutter with the original shaped one. Carefully adjust the depth to match the side pieces already machined.

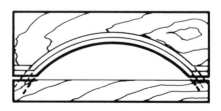

Fig.14.3. Another procedure for shaping top rail of a clock face.

Using a straight narrow long reach cutter, make circular sweeps from left to right until cut straight through.

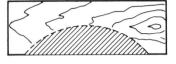

Remove cut-out portion and using the same radius, fit mould cutter in place of straight one.

Make sweeps from left to right until mould form has been achieved.

Tack or clamp straight edge batten to bridge the arc.

Carefully setting cutter position to match the mould, make the straight pass to mould the short tails.

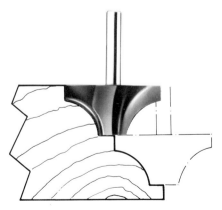

Fig.14.4. By taking two run throughs at different depths, a double ovollo mould was obtained. Cutter Ref. 7/4.

Fig.14.8. The clock face in a more advanced stage of construction.

Fig.14.9. Left can be seen the splendid grandfather clock, the upper part of which was extensively machined with the router, using the hand built trammel device to give special accuracy.

5. Routing aids and templates

Without doubt, it is the use of templates which offers the widest scope of applications for the router. There is literally no limit to the possibilities available, and it is this point which creates a challenge to the craftsman. Commercially it offers the woodworker a fast and efficient means of increasing his output. Template jigs are a more sophisticated means of guiding the router to perform various functions.

Templates are usually made from hardboard, plywood or plastics, the harder the better. Thickness should be between 6mm and 10mm since if they are too thin, there is the possibility of the guide bush slipping out of the template while working, thus spoiling the work. Much ingenuity can be used in the construction of templates, varying the shape and size in accordance with the workpiece. They can be clamped down in a number of ways, by G clamps or toggle clamps or, better still, stuck down with tape. The use of double-sided tape is most effective for this purpose, since the work itself is not marked, and the working area is left completely clear of encumbrances.

There are certain rules to be adopted with the guide bush system, whether an inside or outside template is used. Templates must be cut to size, bearing in mind the space between the guide bush and the cutting edge.

How to assess the size of the template

For the purpose of this exercise, we have chosen a typical application, namely sinking of a flush handle (see Fig. 15). The procedure is as follows:
1.   Choose a cutter of small diameter to match as near as possible the

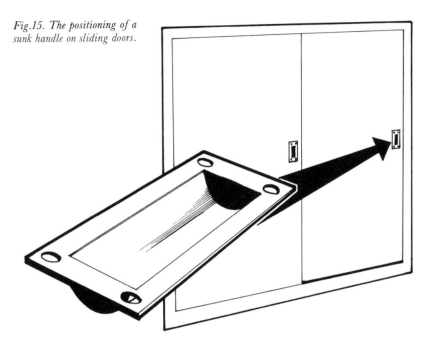

Fig.15. The positioning of a sunk handle on sliding doors.

radius of the corner of the handle (this will reduce the need to clean up the corners with a hand chisel afterwards
2. Choose a guide bush with clearance inside for the cutter to rotate without rubbing. See Fig. 15.1, showing projection of cutter through guide bush.
3. Subtract the diameter of the cutter from the outside diameter of the bush and divide by two. This will indicate how much larger the template should be in relation to the size of the part being recessed. **Refer to Fig. 15.2 for clarification.**
X. This is the outside diameter of the bush.
Y. This is the diameter of the cutter.
Z. This denotes the extra amount to be allowed when cutting out the template.
Special note: The *left* aperture in the template shown in Fig. 15.2 is for recessing the centre deep part of the handle. The right aperture in the template is to recess the outer shallow handle plate.

Fig.15.1. Router, showing guide bush fitted to base. Standard bush supplied is 24mm dia., but other sizes are available.

Fig.15.2. The sketch shows the system for working out the size of the template, relative to the guide bush diameter and cutter diameter.

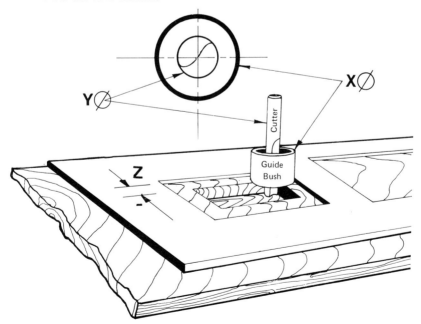

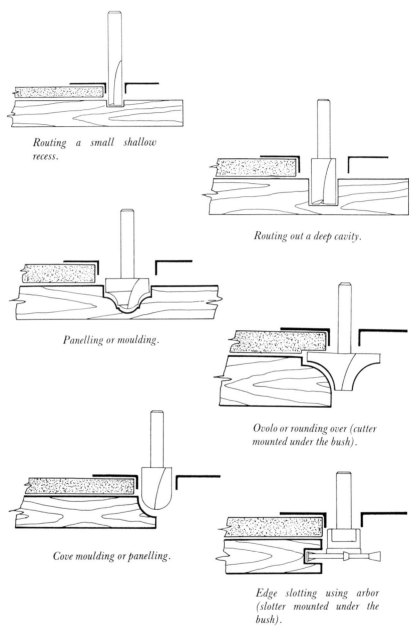

Routing a small shallow recess.

Routing out a deep cavity.

Panelling or moulding.

Ovolo or rounding over (cutter mounted under the bush).

Cove moulding or panelling.

Edge slotting using arbor (slotter mounted under the bush).

Fig.15.3. Six typical guide bush applications described by cross-sectioned sketches.

Types of templates

A variety of template systems will be discussed, some suitable for short runs of work, others intended for batch production in a factory, where speed and maximum output are the priorities. By adopting these professional methods the amateur can extend the use of his router to a surprising degree.

Guide bush selection

Sketch illustrations 15.3 show how the guide bush and template play a valuable part in cutting and shaping to a pattern.

However, the router manufactures only supply a limited number of bush sizes. Fortunately, at least one firm offers a sub-base with a complate range of bushes between 12mm and 30mm diameter.

Large bushes should be used when deep cavities are being cut-out. This allows chips to clear and avoids the 'coffee grinding' effect which causes overheating and burning.

How to apply the router

After the cutter and selected guide bush have been fitted, the router is

Fig.16. (Left) The router base and guide bush, showing the cutter projecting through it.

Fig.16.1. (Right) A template jig for slotting out mortises.

placed on the template surface with the guide bush side pressed against the template edge. The motor is then switched on and the router depressed and locked there. The cutter is now protruding through the centre of the bush to the pre-set depth (see Fig. 16). Now follow the contour of the template, maintaining the pressure of the guide bush against the template edge throughout until work is complete.

A template for mortising

Apart from dovetail joints and dowel joints, mortises and tenons can be effectively cut with the plunge router. A simple template is made and is fitted over the workpiece (Fig. 16.1). A two flute cutter to match the size of the mortise is a natural choice. It is advisable to take several 'bites' to clear swarf and prevent overload. The problem of the rounded corners in the mortise is best solved by rounding the corners of the tenon, but those who prefer a square tenon, can cut the mortise corners square with a chisel. Tenons can be made most efficiently on the router table; see Chapter 8.

Book end shelf unit

We now have a really superb example of template work. The template which is illustrated (Fig. 16.2), plays several roles, for it will enable both housings and apertures to be cut out with one clamping. It can be used for cutting out the heart shaped patterns, and the outside part of the shelf ends.

The template should be made from a close grained hardboard or plastic and secured by doublesided tape.

One minor problem when routing out shapes or small workpieces, is the inclination for the router to tip, due to insufficient support from beneath. The usual procedure is to secure a series of 'pads' around the workpiece at the identical level of the workpiece top. One useful device to overcome this problem, is to use the side fence rods to form a framework on which four adjustable feet provide the level working facility so necessary for such operations. A flat table top surface is essential. See Fig. 16.4 (and 16.5).

When working out template size, remember, the template size

Fig.16.3. This illustration shows book end shelf ready for assembly.

Fig.16.2. The illustration to the left shows template secured to the work-piece by double sided tape. Note, variations in size to allow for the guide bush.

Fig.16.5. Router frame with 'feet' adjusted to obtain identical height to that of template top surface.

must be smaller for the outside portion, and larger for the inside grooving and cutting work. Since the shapes are relatively small, it is advisable to use a narrow diameter cutter, say ¼" Ø, Trend Ref S3/22, and take several bites or passes through the work. This solid carbide cutter stands up well to deep cutting, and is preferable to HSS version because of the abrasive nature of many hardwoods.

If 16mm thick material is chosen, we recommend two 4mm deep cuts for the housings, and four 4mm cuts to reach the full depth of the material and a little beyond. Using this small cutter will enable the router to reach the corners, leaving very little to be square cut with a hand chisel.

Fig.16.6. The finished book end shelf, made in Sapele hardwood, is a prime example of the attractive work produced with the router, extensive use being made of templates.

Recessing handle

Typical home-made template for recessing a drop handle plate.

Using the smaller guide bush and cutter, the deep radius part of the handle is recessed first, and then the template is moved up to allow the shallow part to be routed out.

The radiused corners will need to be squared with a hand chisel.

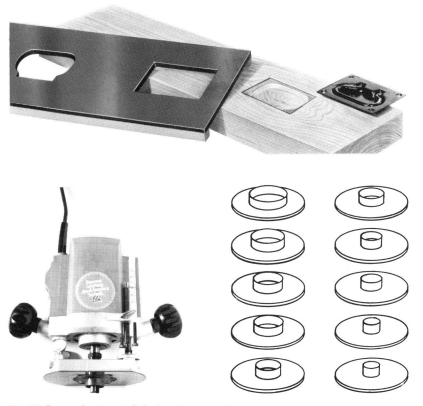

Fig.17. Router showing guide bush with a cutter protruding out of its base.

Bushes are made in various sizes (usually between 10mm and 30mm diameter).

Patchwork with the router

There are thousands of houses needing first aid, in particular, outside joinery, when kiln dried timber is clearly the rogue.

Wet rot in doors, windows and cills can naturally be cut out with hammer and chisel, but a better and more effective method of moving the affected part, is with a plunge router.

The procedure, developed by the Trend Router Division, is to tack a small frame around the rotted portion to be removed. This acts as a template around which the router will be guided from a guide bush on its base. With template in place, the router is plunged in and applied in an anti-clockwise direction, removing a ½" depth of material at a time. The operation takes only a matter of seconds and it offers a clear view of the wood thus acting as a guide for assessing the need to remove further affected timber, by plunging in and taking off another layer. A project is illustrated, Fig. 18.

1) A small frame has been tacked onto the window frame with centre part open for removal of rotted timber using a hand router.

2) The router is seen being used to rout out the rotted portion of timber. This leaves a clean square edge on all faces. By taking out a 12mm depth of material at a time, it is possible to see at a glance how deep one needs to go to reach the sound timber.

(1)   (3)

(2)   (4)

Fig.18.

3) After measuring the size of the aperture, following the removal of rotted wood, an insert, preferably from hardwood, was cut to size and screwed in position.

4) The insert has been fitted. It was first drilled, counterbored, screwed, and cover plugs driven in after screwing.

Box template

For repetition work, when setting-up time needs to be kept to a minimum, a hinged box template can be a useful innovation. It enables the template area to be kept totally clear of encumbrances such as toggle clamps. See Fig. 19. Furthermore, it enables the pattern to be repeatedly routed into a long work-piece, which is moved up to a new position, and re-clamped. The system can be used for panelling effects, or for straight through cutting.

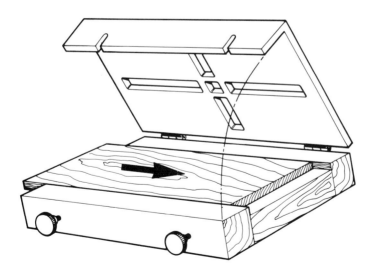

Fig.19. A hinged box template into which a long workpiece can be clamped and moved up to new positions.

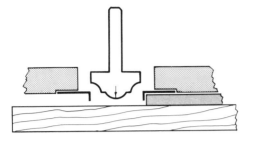

Fig.19.1 Classic panel cutter Ref. 18/51. This was used for the panel shown at Fig. 19.2 but others such as those shown in Fig. 19.3 can also be applied to give a similar effect.

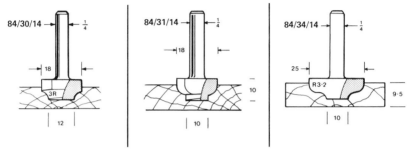

Fig.19.2.

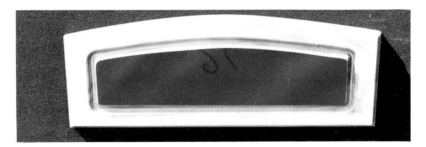

Fig.19.3.

Panelling with a template

Having marked out the shape of central part, a hardboard template was cut to match it (allowance was made for bush diameter). This was affixed with double-sided tape, which rolled off by thumb pressure afterwards. The classic shaped groover chosen was a Ref. 18/51. The depth of cut was checked out first on scrap timber. The router was then set to cut the groove in several passes, not because the router had insufficient power to sustain speed, but to remove burn marks. There is naturally a tendency to hesitate at corners, with resultant burn marks, but a light skim taking off a millimeter of material will remove such marks.

During routing, the guide bush was kept under pressure against the template edge continuously.

Routing convex shapes

The practicality of routing on a convex surface is shown by Fig. 20. A commercial success story hinges around this application.

Access points were needed in large plastic water piping with wall thickness approx. 20mm. To overcome the problem a sub-base to

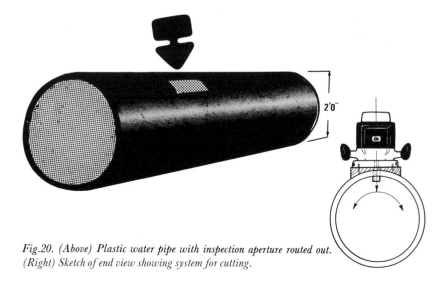

Fig.20. (Above) Plastic water pipe with inspection aperture routed out. (Right) Sketch of end view showing system for cutting.

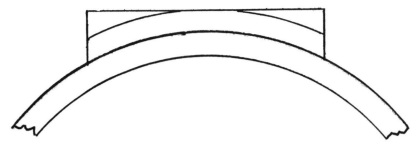

Fig.20.1. Offcut sections of the tube were used to build the matching 'false' base, which was secured to router base with double sided tape.

match the pipe radius was fitted to the existing base. A frame was made to act as a location for the sub-base (see Fig. 20.1).

Then, with a two-step plunge, using an 8mm diam. cutter, a clean opening was cut in less than a minute with a router.

'Sinking' hardware fittings

Cleverly designed factory-made templates can be purchased for production work. These are primarily designed to sink hardware fittings, such as locks, fasteners, and pivots, used in the more sophisticated continental type windows. The one in Fig. 21 has interchangeable panels which clip into place in a matter of seconds. The template frame is available in various forms; it can be clamped onto the surface or onto a door edge for sinking hinges and lock plates.

The interchangeable panels are supplied blank for firms to cut out the shapes they need for recessing their ironmongery. Some progressive ironmongery manufacturers, produce hardware fittings (e.g. hinges) with rounded corners, so no 'cleaning up' of corners with a chisel is needed.

Homemade template for staircase work

A template cut from plywood can be constructed to speed up the cutting out of treads and risers (see Fig. 23). However, great care should be taken in pre-marking out the paths the router will take, as minor discrepancies on the template will multiply by the time the staircase is completed.

Fig.21. This factory-made template jig has interchangeable panels with slots to suit iron-mongery fittings, such as barrel locks, lock plates and window fasteners.

Fig.22. This corner 'clamp-on' template jig has cutting facilities on both the end and side of the door.

Fig.23. Stair housings are routed out with this home-made template device, which is clamped to the workpiece (see Chapter 17, Project B).

Templates for building applications

The cutting out of letter box openings in a 20mm thick plywood panel presents an excellent application for the router. True, it could be done with a drill and jigsaw, but the joy of the router in such an application, is the repetition of a clean cut and accurate finish, with minimal cleaning up required after the job is completed.

Fig. 24 shows a series of letter box openings being cut through a 'master' template, made from duralium. A heavier duty router was used to make the cut out in one pass, but the MOF 96, a smaller version, could have been used for this purpose, making three passes in order to plunge through. Once again the advantages of the plunging action and rotary depth stops come into their own.

Louvred windows and doors

Templates are often used for repetitive grooves, or housings as they are generally termed; making housings for louvres is a typical application. A conventional and craftsmanlike method of setting up to produce louvred housings, is to produce a plywood template, as seen in Fig. 25 which provides a series of stopped grooves. The template is

Fig.24. A heavy duty plunge router is cutting letter box openings. An alloy template is used for the pattern. The template itself was cut out with the router, hence the side fence shown.

(a)

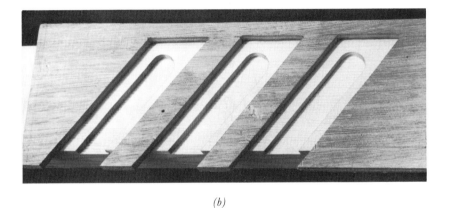

(b)

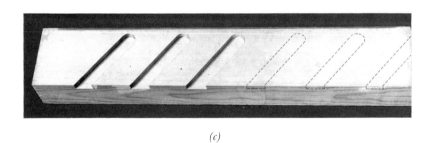

(c)

Fig.25. (a) The template shown was made from ⅜″ thick plywood and panel pinned, in marked out position. (b) Louvre housings have been routed out. Template is ready for moving up to next position. (c) The finished cut housings, routed in sets of three, through template shown in (a). Dotted lines represent the second position of the template.

secured by panel pins or double sided tape. As each set of housings are produced through the template, it is moved to a new position.

Louvre template jig

It is when repetition work is involved that template jigs become an essential aid for production. For high output, the essence of the problem is to produce as many identical housings as possible in a given time. One method of achieving higher production is to use a sliding box template, on the lines sketched in Fig. 25.1.

Fig.25.1. For making louvred doors, a sliding 'box' template provides a useful means for routing out the end housings at predetermined spacings.

Fig.26. Attractive shapes being routed through an 'inside' template.

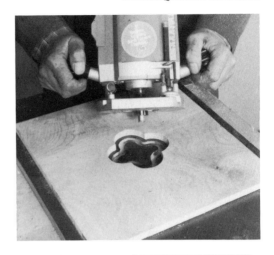

Fig.26.1. Pattern being copied by using 'outside' template.

Fig.26.2. Using a simple rectangular template, preferably made from hard plastic material, panelling can be produced with attractive results. By using different radiused cutters, a variety of effects can be achieved.

Artistic shapes

With the Elu router portrayed here, a number of sizes of guide bushes are available (see Fig. 17). These, in conjunction with inside cutting or outside cutting templates, offer numerous possibilities, particularly of an artistic nature. Attractive panels and cut-outs can be produced when making chairs, desks, and cupboards, etc. Two examples are shown in Figs. 26 and 26.1.

Panelling work on say, cupboard doors, is a typical use for simple rectangular templates (see Fig. 26.2). Using some of the latest Ovolo, Ogee and Classic shaped cutters (see Chapter 17), unusual and attractive effects can be obtained. By alternating the guide bushes and cutters, intricate mould shapes can be produced.

6. Routing jigs and devices

Drilling through a template

We have seen how dowel drilling can be performed with a template jig. Likewise larger holes for recessing circular hinges, and sink taps can be drilled in the same manner. Illustration 27.1, shows a laminated vanity basin top with central part routed out and holes 20mm diam. drilled out.

The template which was made from Masonite hardboard, included apertures to accept the 30mm guide bush fitted on the router base.

By substituting the 8mm diam. TC cutter, used for the central part,

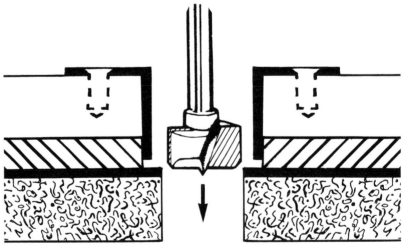

Fig.27. A clean cut drilled hole is achieved by the plunge router, using a 20mm diam. Ref. 421 TC machine bit.

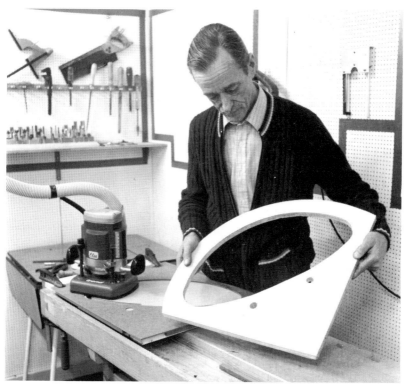

Fig.27.1. Vanity basin top has been cut out with a router through a template. Note the tap fitting holes which have been 'router drilled'. Router was fitted with a dust extraction hood, and connected to a 150 C.F.M. extraction unit.

with a 20mm one, preferably the type 421, illustrated Fig. 27, drilled holes for the tap fittings, are cut in a matter of seconds. Furthermore router drilled holes are clean cut and free from chipping-out at entry part.

Note the dust extraction hood which was fitted to the router in this operation, in order to obtain a dust-free working environment.

Stop groove beading jig

One more example of the fascinating possibilities for the router, is a bead jig. (Figs 28–28.3.)

Fig.28. A finished length of bead made from a series of stop grooves cut from opposing sides.

Fig.28.1. The router runs in a 'track' to a preset cut depth and length.

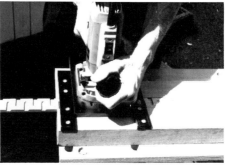

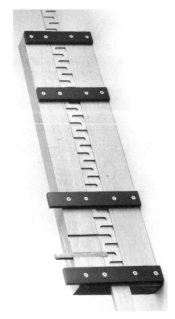

Fig.28.2. (Above) The sub-base allows adjustment when screwed to the router base. The stop has an opening to allow the locator peg to enter.

Fig.28.3. (Left) The grooving jig showing the locating peg which is slipped into each preceeding groove.

Relatively simple to make; with this device, one can convert a thin wood batten into an attractive edge bead, with a most professional finish.

Similar in principal to the 'cross hatch' jig, the material is fed along a controlled path within the jig. The router is applied at 90 deg. to form a series of stop grooves. The workpiece is reversed and cuts made from the opposite side.

To ensure the pattern is exact, with slots equivalent, a dovetail peg is slid into each preceeding slot. It is not hammered into place.

A sub-base, made from plastic or plywood, has length adjusting slots and a stop at one end. The base slides between two guides and ensures exact matching grooves.

'Cross hatch' jigs

There are numerous ways of cutting intricate patterns and moulds into a surface panel, but a 'cross hatch' jig has special merit.

If the router owner is prepared to take the trouble and make such a device, diamond shaped patterns and panelling of totally original design can be formed by interchanging cutters and varying the depth and width. There is wide scope for artistic design.

The jig is illustrated in Fig. 28.5.

The construction of the jig, made entirely from wood or plywood, is based on a sliding 'track', which allows the work-piece to slide across the routing path in predetermined increments. An angular 90 deg. 'bridge' is secured to the framework. It offers two 45 deg. routing paths across the workpiece, from two directions.

For the purpose of this exercise, the grooves were spaced at 20mm apart. A sliding 'peg' locates in each preceding groove and ensures identical spacings. Two cutters were used to obtain the panelling effect illustrated. First cut was made with a two flute cutter. Ref 3/4 8mm diam. cutting depth was 10mm. This was followed by a radius cutter ref 13/2 diam. 18mm, cutting depth was 8mm.

Adjustable jig/template

A modular framing device, comprising of a range of slotted

Fig.28.4. The router in passed across the frame, cutting a mould into the central sliding member. This is moved up and pegged to a new position.

Fig.28.5. A top view of the cross-hatch jig, showing the system for cross grooving and clamping.

Fig.28.6. A close up view of one attractive panelling effect.

aluminium components, can be adjusted to form squares, rectangles or hexagons. Described as the 'Jigmaster', (Fig. 28.8) this system is based on square tubes, with elongated slots, to enable them to bolt together to form an enclosure for the router to circumvent. If the router base is not round, a round sub-base must be fitted. The purpose of the device is to provide a flexible template, and/or guide for routing

Fig.28.7. A further attractive diamond shaped pattern, using an ogee mould on a wider spacing.

Fig.28.8. This adjustable template is made from slotted aluminium square tube. It's modular design offers square, rectangular or octagonal shapes by interchanging the components.

square patterns (Fig. 28.7). For template work, the usual calculations need to be made to find the relative size of template opening. i.e. distance from cutter edge to outside edge of round base.

Peg frame jig – see Fig. 28.8

For square cross hatching, a 'peg' frame jig shows certain advantages. (Fig. 28.9.)

With this jig, a series of grooves can be cut equidistant, and by reversing and grooving across the grain on the back of the board, most attractive patterns emerge – see Fig. 28.10.

The jig illustrated was made from ⅜" thick Tufnol, a hard dense plastic but could easily be constructed from plywood. Dowel pegs carefully spaced and inserted at 90 deg. form the basis of the jig. The frame, which is constructed from four components, is collapsable, and adjustable in size to accept different size workpieces.

The system for using the jig is based on cutting a series of parallel grooves, with guide fence locating on the dowel pegs at either end. See Fig. 28.8. Cuts are made across the grain first, then along the grain on the reverse side.

By varying the size and shape of cutters used in the router, totally original patterns are made. For this exercise, a radiused cutter, 16mm diam. was used Ref. 13/1. (Fig. 28.11.)

Fig.28.8.

Fig.28.9. This peg frame is adjustable, and enables a series of parallel grooves to be routed on both sides of the wood panel.

Fig.28.10. One example of an attractive mesh pattern produced on the peg frame. Material was Parana Pine. A cross grain series of cuts were made at 90° on the reverse side, in order to obtain the mesh effect.

Fig.28.11. Ref. 13/1 radius cutter was used on both sides of workpiece.

Decorative edge strips – see Fig. 28.12

Having found the means of cross grooving with various devices just described there is a simple means of cutting square edged beading in a fraction of the time normally taken by a jigsaw or bandsaw. Groove a series of square slots *along* the grain at equal distance from each other. If narrow slivers are cut *across* the grain, an effect is produced as shown in Fig. 28.12.

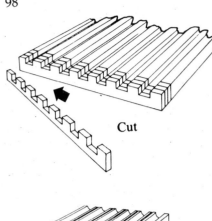

Cut

Fig.28.12. To make square cut slotted beading, first cut equal distant grooves along the grain and then cut slivers across the grain. grain.

Edge strips used to head the ramparts of a model castle.

Fig.28.13. Cove moulding strips can be routed by cutting a series of radiused grooves, and then cutting the panel into strips longitudinally.

By grooving ovolo, ogee, and classic style shapes, some interesting and unique patterns can emerge.

Long-radial cuts will produce attractive mouldings too.

'Cross-hatch' jigs can be made to facilitate the cutting of the grooves to exact spacings (Fig. 28.5).

Producing cove mouldings – see Fig. 28.13

One useful means of producing moulded strips, is to rout a series of radiused grooves (using group 12 or 13 cutters), at equal distances from one another. The material is then sawn into strips. See 28.13.

Column fluting jig

The Jig described here, is basically of quite simple construction but as the designer explained, there was no need for an elaborate device to produce this fine pair of columns for his fireplace. See Fig. 29.1.

The indexing disc for marking the end of the pillar. ▶

Fig.29. The pillar is seen in the box jig, which pinned the pillar centrally for tuning in 1/12 indexed stages. Router was fitted with side fence. End stops were clamped at either end (removed for clarity).

The router used, was a 650 Watt, plunge type. The cutter fitted (see Fig. 29.2) was a ref. 13/2 cutter giving a 9mm radiused fluting. The jig was made from chipboard off-cuts, and consisted of a base, two sides and ends, screwed together.

The column was initially turned smooth, and two holes, 8mm dia. were drilled dead centre at both ends. Two 8mm projecting rods were mounted exactly at 90° from blocks fitted within the box structure.

The indexing system was first worked out geometrically, after careful deliberation about number of flutes, also size and depth of grooves. A circular card with index markings (see Fig. 29) was used to transpose the index spacings on to the end of the pillar. The position for each routing pass was gauged from a datum line seen on the end of the jig, which lined up with the 12 index markings on the pillar extremity. (Each mark corresponding with one flute.) A screw

Fig.29.1. The pair of completed pillars with end caps which had been turned on a lathe.

Fig.29.2. A 13/2 cutter is used to cut a 9mm radiused groove.

was inserted from the end support, to secure the pillar at each indexed position. Guidance of the router along the length of the pillar had naturally to be precise, although Mr. Ralph Fellows the designer and maker of the fireplace, only used a standard side fence. However, this gentleman is highly skilled, and the author advises the amateur not to take chances. Preferably build a double track or fence so the router cannot depart from its exact path. Make test runs first taking shallow cuts. End limit stops were fitted in appropriate positions, but not illustrated for reasons of clarity.

Extrusion jig for cutting and drilling aluminium

One of the thriving and growing facets of the building trade has been the introduction of aluminium extrusions for door and window construction. It has been the use of plunging type routing techniques which have made the fabrication work so economical. Without such innovations, the construction with extrusions would be extremely labour intensive.

The machine shown in Fig. 30 is the clamp-on routing jig, and is just one of a number of such machines which vary in sophistication and output. This machine, namely the Elu Ref SAL 54, is ideally for batch production runs in window and door construction. Whilst home made templates can be made for these applications, generally speaking the standard of work produced from them is inferior. Machining of aluminium and other non-ferrous metals requires complete rigidity of both template and workpiece. The principle on which these clamp on machines work is as follows:

A metal template to match the slots required is fitted within the framework. In operation the routing jig is fitted over the aluminium window or door and clamped, using the special eccentric clamp provided and gauging the position with the side or length stops. The router is then switched on and depressed so that the cutter penetrates the workpiece. When the router is locked in position it is guided along the sliding framework (laterally and transversely) until the cut is completed. The knob is then given a quarter turn anti-clockwise, to enable the router head to spring out of the work.

This routing device is extremely efficient and fast in operation. It is powered by a single-phase, 600 Watt motor, with a free running speed of 20,000 rpm. A more automated machine which produces a higher output is also now available. The ideal machining speed is approx. 12,000 rpm and models with variable speeds between 8,000 and 20,000 rpm, can now offer this facility. Certainly at the higher speed, more attention to methods of coolant is advisable.

A number of cutters are available for machining aluminium (these are illustrated in the Appendix, ref. groups 47/2, 47/20, 50). Most of them have single spiral geometry, and are capable of drilling, slotting and profiling aluminium extrusions in one operation. These cutters, made from special high speed steel, are ideal for recessing keyholes and hardware fittings when used at speeds between 10,000 and 24,000 rpm.

It is recommended that a lubricant stick is applied to the workpiece, or a mist spray to the cut, during operation. In this way, a clean burr free cut can be achieved. Certainly, attention to such details will extend the life of the cutters.

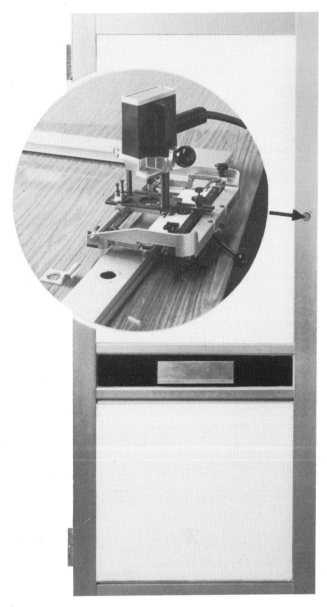

Fig.30. Slotting holes and keyways in aluminium frames is just one more job for the Plunge Router. The machine shown is an Elu model SAL 54. It is only a 2 minute operation to slot and drill the extrusion ready to receive the lockset.

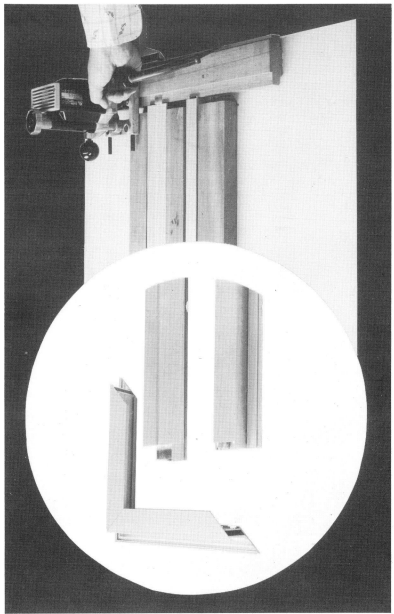

Fig.30.1. Transom cutter in action, cutting the end of an extrusion.

Cutting aluminium transoms

Using the router in the way illustrated, trimming the ends of extrusions for producing transoms and mullions can be undertaken most efficiently. It should be mentioned that this is an inexpensive way of producing machined end sections, there being more sophisticated machinery to cut transoms on a production basis. The hand equipment, described here, consists of a hand powered router, supplied as a set which includes hard wood runners, into which the extrusions slide, a cross runner bar, toggle clamps to hold the material, and a special tungsten carbide tipped router cutter, which is designed to rebate the extrusion ends, leaving a clean cut finish (Fig. 30.1). (The cutter is illustrated in Chapter 17.) The action is fast, and no cleaning up is required.

Fig.30.2. A home-made template set up for clamping and slotting the extrusions.

Slotting and drilling aluminium

While there is a special purpose-made jig for cutting slots in extrusions, a home-made template with clamps and guides, similar in some respects to the transom set-up, can be used to drill and slot, e.g. for making keyholes and recesses to accept lock plates (see Fig. 30.2). The sections should be held rigid if vibration and the consequential poor finish is to be avoided.

Router/lathe workshop

A most productive and creative device is now available to extend the use of hand routers. It is generally described as a router/lathe onto which light duty routers (maximum 6lbs) can be clamped in place. In Fig. 31 the Elu MOF 96 router is shown clamped onto a router/lathe. The depth adjustment knob is an important feature, since fine adjustment of height and steady feed-in is necessary to obtain a good finish. The separate components of the router/lathe can be seen in Fig. 31.1. The workpiece, which commences as a square section of wood, is fitted between tailstock and headstock. The hand router is fitted by bolts to

Fig.31. The Elu MOF 96 router is seen fitted to the 'Woodmaster'. Note the depth adjustment knob for fine adjustment of height, a most important feature for lathe cutting work, as a steady feed-in is necessary to obtain a good finish. The 600 watt motor of the Elu router allows for a relatively heavy cut to be made in one pass.

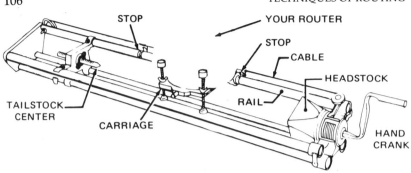

Fig.31.1. The router/lathe is illustrated with the main features described. The workpiece, which commences as a square section of wood, is fitted between tailstock and the headstock. The hand router is fitted by bolts to the carriage. Adjustable stops limit the lateral stroke to suit applications, the carriage sliding on the two uppermost rails. The hand crank turns the workpiece and, if the index pin is engaged, the carriage slides simultaneously along the guide rails.

the carriage. Adjustable stops limit the lateral stroke to suit applications, the carriage sliding on the two uppermost rails. The hand crank turns the workpiece, and if the index pin is engaged, the carriage slides simultaneously along the guide rails. The indexing head is illustrated fully in Fig. 31.2 to show the scale setting.

Three basic operations can be performed: turning; lateral fluting and beading; and a combination of fluting, cutting and turning.

In turning operations the workpiece is rotated by the cranked

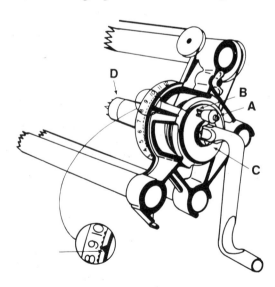

Fig.31.2. A=indexing pin. B = slot to receive index pin. C = drum housing which houses cable. D = spiked engaging head (this is removed and driven into workpiece centre point).

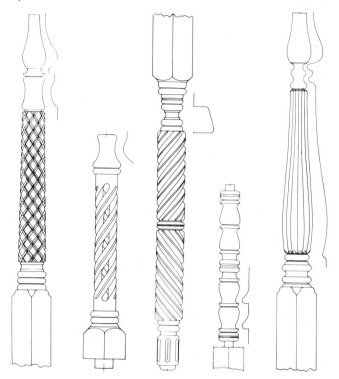

Fig.31.3. A number of attractive shaped legs. The lines adjacent to some of the drawings show the shape required if a template pattern is used.

handle. The routing machine is manually slid along the carriage (with an optional template for working to a pre-shaped pattern).

Lateral grooving may be carried out in 24 different positions, utilising the indexing head which is located within the headstock.

By using a combination of the above two operations spiral and 'roping' patterns can be obtained. In this instance the indexing head is used together with the auto-cable drive. Cranking the handle turns the workpiece and drives the carriage along the slides simultaneously. These spiral and roping cuts are done in multiples of 12, 8, 6 or 4 equidistant passes through 360 deg. In this way most attractive chair or table legs can be produced (see Fig. 31.3).

Routing aids

Standard accessories offerred with the router, and even those purchased separately, have their limitations.

There is therefore much scope for the router owner to produce some of his own routing aids.

Certain devices shown in this book are likely to be available commercially in due course, but innovation in one's own workshop, is most satisfying.

Equipment described, can be broadly divided into categories; templates, jigs, clamps and guides.

Template materials

There are a number of options for those making their own templates. However, the most reliable ones should have the following properties. They should be rigid, hard and not too brittle. For guidance, we shall list the materials available.

Natural wood
Hard softwoods, and dense hardwoods, both make good templates, but the problem of finding large thin sheets can be a setback.

Man-made boards
Hardboard – Not recommended unless you can obtain the very dense variety. e.g. Masonite.
Plywood-Dense high grade plywood makes quite good templates. If laminated covered, so much the better.
Chipboard – Not suitable
Blockboard – Not suitable

Plastics
The variety of plastic sheeting is rather bewildering but avoid PVC and Polypropylene
Acrylic Material – e.g. Perspex, Plexiglas and Oraglas has its merits, but it is inclined to crack, being rather brittle.
Hard Resinous Plastics-Bakelite, Wareite, Formica and Tufnol are proven to be the best materials from experience. Tufnol is the favourite for two reasons. Firstly, it machines better, giving out chips

rather than dust, and it can be obtained in convenient thicknesses, which leads us to the next point.

Thickness of template

A template should be as thin as possible, but above 6mm for safety. Remember, only a slight movement could cause the bush to slip out of place. The ideal thickness is between 6mm and 10mm. Above 10mm, there will be an inclination to restrict the cutting depth. So when considering the template to be used, check the projection of bush and cutter.

Clamping systems

When routing, and especially when template work is involved. The workpiece, template, and guides may all need to be fixed or clamped in some way.
We shall list the alternatives:

Quick-action clamps, Fig. 32.2
These are invaluable for temporary clamping materials quickly and securely. They are available in a variety of sizes.

Toggle clamps, Fig. 32.2
Available in a number of sizes. When a permanent clamping position is needed, the toggle clamp has special merit.

Double sided tape, Fig. 32.3
Clamping with D.S.T. is highly recommended for template applications. The working area can be kept entirely free from encumbrances and projections. Providing the surfaces being clamped with D.S.T., are smooth, (wood being planes), it is an invaluable aid for all router users.
D.S.T. should have a rubber based adhesive, with a 'peel off' edge to offer quick applications.

After use, the components can be prised apart and the D.S.T. rolls off with thumb pressure quite easily. Ask for template grade when purchasing.

Other holding devices

Eccentric clamp, Fig. 32.4
These are normally hand made from some hard material 8mm to 12mm thick. Sketch below shows the system of engaging the clamp. The central pivot point should be just off centre. It is important that the screw or bolt must be large and very well secured, as the pressure exerted will wrench the screw out.

A further point to remember is that the material being clamped must have a stop at the end to prevent the clamp from moving the workpiece in the 'pivot direction' – see sketch for clarification.

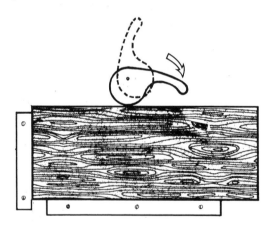

Wedge clamp, Fig. 32.5
This simple form of clamping can be applied when long parallel sections need to be clamped fast for machining.

A good example of this clamping system is shown in Fig. 32.5. The workpieces are held firmly by the two wedges in the top of a louvre Template Jig.

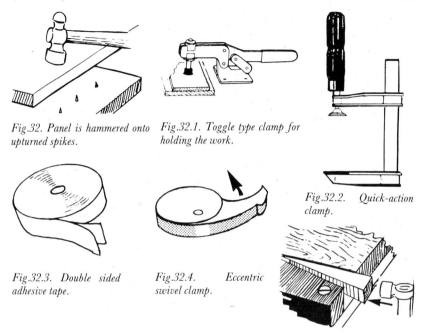

Fig.32. Panel is hammered onto upturned spikes.

Fig.32.1. Toggle type clamp for holding the work.

Fig.32.2. Quick-action clamp.

Fig.32.3. Double sided adhesive tape.

Fig.32.4. Eccentric swivel clamp.

Fig.32.5. Drive-in wedge.

Upturned nails, Fig. 32

If nail marks are acceptable, then workpieces needing moderate clamping against side thrust, can be held by upturned nails.

Vacuum clamping

This is a lengthy subject, and is dealt with quite fully in chapter 13.

Routing Base Plates

When routing parallel grooves, the router is often not well balanced, relative to gripping and handling.

If a long sub-base is screwed on to the existing base of the router, and grip handles bolted at either end (see Fig. 33) a comfortable and useful accessory is obtained, at very little cost. Base material can be made from plywood, or hard plastic for longer life. Handles can be obtained from a good tool or D.I.Y. shop.

On some hand routers, an extension for the standard base can be mounted on the standard guide rods, supplied with the machine. See

Fig.33. This sub-base made from hard plastic can be fitted to all hand router bases. Grip knobs can be obtained from a good tool shop.

Fig.33.1. One can obtain extra purchase on the router with a base fitted with grip handles.

Fig.33.2. This grip handle device will fit straight onto the two standard guide rods of the router.

Fig. 33.2. This system is even better from one point of view, in that no loss of cutter depth is involved whatsoever.

Adjustable guide jig

Whilst the usual guides are simple and made from battens a 'universal' guiding devices can be constructed using a saw and router, components being ready available from offcuts. Alternatively, it can be obtained complete, ready for use, at a moderate price.

Fig.34. Guide jig. For making housings, the guide jig is clamped across the workpiece with a slot in centre to accommodate the guide bush on the router. Stop grooves can be cut by clamping end stops to the end members.

Fig.34.1. Alternative set-up, when the router base itself is passed within the two side members.

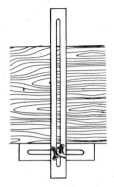

When a short member is clamped to a long one, at 90°, a useful T square is formed.

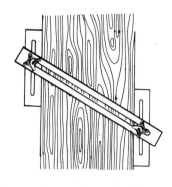

When two short members and one long one are clamped at 45°, a useful angle guide is formed.

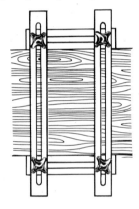

When two short and two long members are clamped across the workpiece, the space between the long bars can accommodate the router base for guidance purposes.

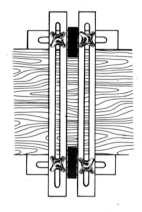

Similarly, when long guide members are closed up to allow guide bush of router to slide along within the slot, the router is held on an exact path. Note the end limit stops for stop grooves on housings.

The guiding system works on a basically simple concept, namely the flexible pivoting of parallel bars, which are clamped in different combinations.

Basic construction: It comprises two pairs of Tufnol bars, 10mm thick, one pair 300mm long, the other, 600mm long. Four strong grip knobs with coach bolts, and nuts. (See Fig. 34.)

Purpose of the guide jig

This device offers a multi-purpose range of applications. For marking out and preparing the work for cutting, routing and drilling, the jig is assembled in different combinations, e.g. to form a T square, box and angle guides, the guide jig not only acts as a guide fence for routing, but also for template work. For housings, the guiding facility is attractive because the problem with the normal fence, is that the router can run off course, through operator error or just inexperience.

With this device, the guides can be adjusted to close up and allow the guide bush on the router base to slide between the bars. In this way, the router cannot run off course and spoil the work. Alternatively, the bars can close up either side of the router base in order to prevent the same possibility. For stop grooving, limit stops in plywood can be bolted to the end members. Templates can be formed by box framing. Alternatively, a separate template frame can be held within the perimeters of the guide bars. In both cases, the advantage of not requiring inner clamps to retain the template or drilling jig in place, is fairly obvious. It leaves the working area free from encumbrances. The Jig and workpiece must naturally be clamped to the work table from both sides, but at points where they do not hinder the router's path, preferably at the corners.

Parallel routing guide

Some routing bases, lend themselves to valuable adaptions for router owners, who wish to improve their equipment. The base illustrated at Fig. 34.2, has been fitted with a 'tracking fence', which slots into a grooved board. It ensures, the router grooves an exact path, with no possibility of router running off course.

The device consists basically, of a pair of linkage sets which bolt onto one standard guide rod projecting from the router base. A narrow section of 8mm hard plastic is secured to the linkage points. In operation, the plastic fence locates into an 8mm routed groove along the full length of a plywood board, thus forming a mono-track. If candle wax or soap is applied within the groove, the fence will slide effortlessly along the track.

Fig.34.2. The router is seen fitted with a sliding side fence, which runs in a track to avoid any movement off the routing path.

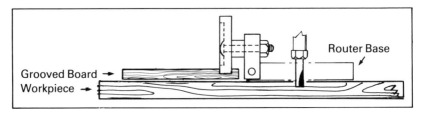

Fig.34.3. Cross section of routing guide showing the basic construction.

7.   Trimming plastics

Those who have tried trimming Formica edges by hand will know how difficult it is to obtain a professional finish. In this chapter we shall describe how the Elu router can carry out such work at considerable speed and leave a clean cut edge with no cleaning up being required whatsoever.

Trimming the edge (vertical) lips first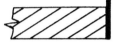

For straight edges, it is the normal practice to use narrow strips of plastic to form the edge lippings. These should be glued in place, preferably allowing no more than 3mm of the edge to project above the board edge.

It is important that the edge strip should be glued and trimmed *before* the top sheet is fitted. This will ensure that the top plastic surface is not marked or spoilt by the under edge of the cutter when trimming the lips flush with the board top. See Figs 35 and 35.1.

Setting up the router for edge trimming (vertical edge)

The fine vertical adjuster is fitted to the router (in lieu of the depth rod), and engaged by the threaded screw on the rotary depth stop. A suitable cutter for trimming the lipping is shown in the Appendix. It has a bottom cut as well as a side cut, enabling it to be used for trimming the overlay, which is discussed overleaf.

The adjuster disengages the plunge spring action, and if it is rotated clockwise, the cutter will plunge deeper. Depth is set just to skim along the (uncovered) top surface, with the centre of the cutter aligned over the vertical lipping (see Fig. 35). Before actually commencing to trim the lipping, make a test run on a piece of scrap wood, with an off-cut of plastic fitted to it (secured by double-sided tape). With practice this procedure becomes unnecessary, but at first a little experience is essential. Remember to cut in clockwise direction for trimming vertical edge. This prevents chipping out.

Fig.35. Trimming the vertical lipping, using the side fence and depth adjuster to gauge the correct amount to remove.

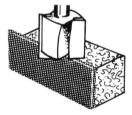

Fig.35.1. The T.C. trimming cutter has a special base cutting edge to give a clean cutting finish Ref. 47/2 90° cut.

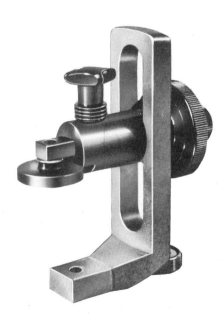

Fig.35.2. The larger router is seen trimming vertical lipping, using the lateral roller adjuster and the latest vertical fine adjuster which offers 'micro' feed. Note that vertical lipping should be trimmed with router being passed in clockwise direction. This will prevent chipping and breakouts. A stepped base plate was fitted to give clearance for the projecting lip. Once more the 47/2 90° bottom trim cutter was utilised.

Fig.35.3. (Left) This fine lateral 'screw feed' offers fine adjustment when exact position for trimming is required. The 'guide' roller follows the board edge – ideal for trimming shaped table tops, etc.

Preparing for trimming the overlay top

Assuming the vertical lipping has been trimmed flush with the top surface, the overlay on the plastic top is now ready for fitting. The procedure is as follows:

The laminate sheet is cut and glued in place with approximately ⅛in. overhang. Excess glue should be removed, as this could become a hindrance when cutting. Once the glue has hardened, the edge can be trimmed back. Assuming a 90 deg. cut edge is required, a square edged tungsten tipped cutter is fitted to the router. This should be cutter ref. 47/2, the bottom edge of which was used to trim the lipping.

While the vertical adjuster is still left in position and used to bring the cutting edge down to the required position, the fine adjuster on the side fence is all important for trimming the top surface correctly. This will provide the means of obtaining that close trimmed edge, so important for a really professional finish.

Trimming the overlay

The machine is positioned over the work and the cutter brought down until the face of the cutting edge lines up with the laminate surface. The side adjuster gives the final position but until experience has been obtained in setting up, it is a good plan to make some trial runs to ensure that the machine is set correctly. Trim from left to right as shown in Fig. 35.4.

Combined trimming and slotting

A slot can be made in the edge of a table top or sideboard at the same time as the overlay is trimmed (see Fig. 35.5). Assuming the plastic top has not been trimmed, cutter ref. 47/1 has the facility to trim the edge at 90 deg., and slot the edge simultaneously to accept a 'keyed' or barbed edge strip. The slotter is bolted to its base in much the same way as the slotter is fitted to the 33/6 arbor. It is necessary to make some trial runs to ensure the slot is central. Edge strips should be tight fitting and gently tapped into position with a mallet after glueing (see Fig. 35.6). It is advisable to choose an undersize slotter (one size below tongue thickness).

Fig.35.4. Trimming the plastic overlay, using the side fence and fine lateral adjuster to bring the cutter in parallel with the underlying edge.

Fig.35.5. Trimming the overlay and slotting the board edge simultaneously is now possible. A special trimming set is available for this purpose. The Elu MOF 31 is seen performing this operation on a 'kidney' shaped coffee table. Cutter Ref. 47/1 is being used with slotter Ref. SL/E.

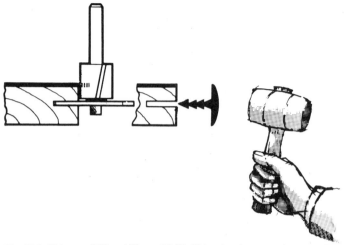

Fig.35.6. Trimmer 47/1 and Slotter SL/C. This trimming cutter has a combination facility. It will trim and slot a recess for a 'barbed' edge strip, which is then tapped into the slot.

Combination Trimming at various angles

There is often preferance for the laminate edge to be clearly defined. This is done by bevelling the edges. For this purpose a range of cutters is available. One useful cutter will trim the vertical lipping at 90°, and have facility to cut the overlay lipping at 45° or 90°. See Fig. 35.7.

Trimming shaped panels

Trimming the lips of shaped panels can present a problem, but a special trimming cutter is available for this purpose. Fig. 35.8 shows a table top being trimmed with a trimmer ref. 46/2. This cutter has a

Fig.35.7. Cutter set disassembled. Refer to Chapter 17 showing range of slotters in SL/A–SL/H group.

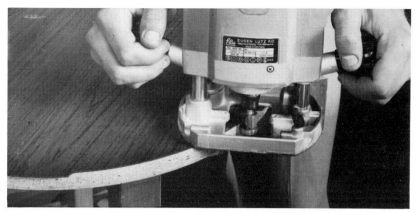

Fig.35.8. Trimming the plastic overlay on this table top, presents no problem, if a trimmer with guide roller type 46/2 is used. The surface edge of board should be smooth, as imperfections could be reflected in the plastic edge.

bearing mounted on its base, the same diameter as the cutter. By dispensing with the side fence, the roller on the cutter follows the shape of the panel and the cutter above it trims the laminate cleanly and accurately. Note, however, that the board edges should be smooth, since any imperfections will be reflected in the laminate edge.

Panels faced on both sides

When boards are faced on both sides with laminate, the edges can be speedily flushed with a trimmer which is designed to cut both edges simultaneously. The cutter is made in two parts, with a bearing guide in the centre

Cutting out 'pockets' in the overlay (see Fig. 35.9)

Inset sinks and basins obviously need apertures to accept soap dishes, wastes, taps or overflows. The normal procedure is to first cut out the apertures in the underlying board, glue the plastic overlay down and then cut out the 'pockets' under the laminate covering. The means of doing this, with the plunge router, is to 'pierce' drill the laminate over the pocket, and cut out the aperture using cutter type ref. 47/4. Fig. 35.9

Fig.35.9. A plunge and trim TC cutter is being used to cut out 'pockets' of laminate. The cutter has a follower on its base to ensure that the cutter follows the correct path.

shows the action of this cutter which cuts the laminate, using the smooth end part of the cutter to follow the shape of the underlying board.

Tips for extending cutter life

The projection of the overhang of laminate should be minimal, as overhang in excess of 3mm can cause cutter wear to increase by as much as 400 per cent. The sketches in Fig. 35.11 show how to avoid unnecessary cutter wear.

Another tip which gives longer life from the cutters is to adjust the depth of the cutter regularly when trimming the laminate top surface. In this way it is possible to spread the wear on the cutter most effectively. Fig. 35.12 shows this recommendation clearly.

Trimmers when side fence will be needed.

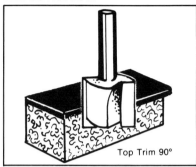

Trimmer Ref. 47/2
Trims top and lipping at 90%

Trimmer Ref. 47/7
Trims edges at 90% and 60% also
lipping at 90%.

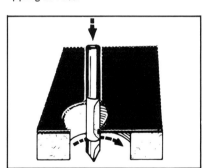

Pierce and Trim. Ref. 47/4
Plunges through and trims laminate
'Pocket'.
Fig.35.10.

Self-guide trimmers with roller bearing guides.

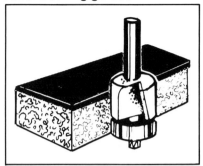

Self–guided Trimmer Ref. 46/2
Trims top overlay at 90% following
board edge.

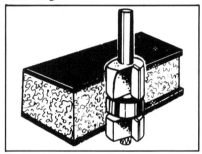

Self–guiding Double Trimmer
Ref. 46/7
Trims top and bottom edges of
laminate simultaneously.

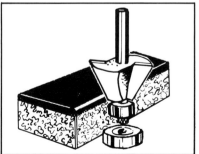

Self–guided Bevel Trimmer
Ref. 46/3 – 46/6
Trims top at 80%, 60%, 45% and 30%

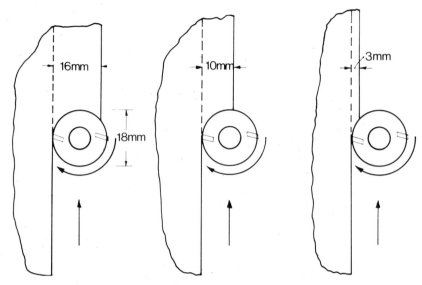

Fig.35.11. If you limit the projection of the plastic edge, so a minimum of material is removed, this will drastically extend the life of the cutter. Left to right, incorrect — better — correct.

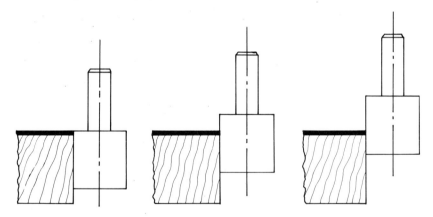

Fig.35.12. Useful tip to extend the life of cutters: a longer life for the cutting edges can be obtained if the trimming depth is varied. Introducing bevel trimmers at different heights will also spread the wear of the cutting edges.

8. Joints and tenons

Dovetail joint

A dovetail joint is usually recommended as the most secure one. To test this claim a colleague and I performed an interesting experiment. Using a small dovetail cutter (ref. 31/2), a six-inch-long dovetail groove was cut in a Sapele hardwood block. Then a dovetail tongue to match the groove was made in a section of chipboard, using the same

Fig.36. A dovetailed slide is not just attractive, but efficient and immensely strong.

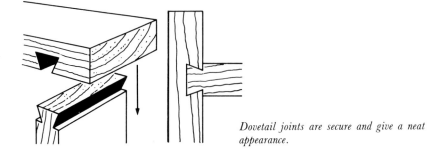

Dovetail joints are secure and give a neat appearance.

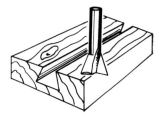

Fig.36.1. A 15° (105° outside) dovetail cutter. Cutter Ref. 31/2.

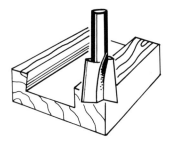

Fig.36.2. This dovetail cutter used in staircase construction has a 5° angle (95° outside). Cutter Ref. 32/10.

cutter. The fine adjuster on the side fence was used to obtain the exact width needed.

The dovetail tongue was then slid into the dovetail groove using hand pressure only. The block was then attached to a ceiling joist and my colleague, 10 stone in weight, lifted himself off the ground. The joint was examined afterwards, and no stress or fatigue break-away, was apparent. Clearly a dovetail joint, even without glue, nails or screw fixings, provides a most secure means of jointing one piece of material to another. An added advantage is that framework, shelving and the like, can be disassembled; a useful asset when moving house.

Fig.36.3. Top face of guides must be really flat with all edges parallel.

Fig.36.4. Dovetail tongue is seen being cut, using a set of parallel guides to guage the spacing for the two half dovetail grooves on the workpiece.

Dovetail guide set

Cutting the dovetail tongue evenly, and effectively, so as to obtain a good fit, can be a 'hit or miss' affair, unless a guiding device is adopted.

Here is one proven guiding system, which will enable one to cut the tongue evenly from both sides.

Construction is based on two identical angular boards which fit in between the vice jaws on the workbench.

These members must have both faces meeting at 90° and top guide bars must be of identical width. The workpiece is vertically mounted and clamped between the two members, with top faces parallel. See Fig. 36.5. The two outer sides of the members will act as guides against which the side fence of the router will run. The router is set to the depth of the dovetail groove.

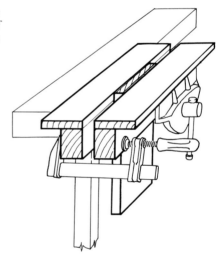

Fig.36.5. (Right) dovetail tongue is cut by fitting two angular guides within jaws of vice. Two passes of router are needed, i.e. up right side and return from opposing end.

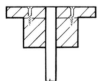

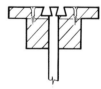

Fig.36.6. Pair of identical guides are clamped flush and parallel within jaws of vice. Board is ready for dovetailing

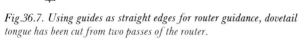

Fig.36.7. Using guides as straight edges for router guidance, dovetail tongue has been cut from two passes of the router.

The routing procedure is as follows:

The first cut is made in anti-clockwise direction, along right hand side of workpiece, and second cut along right hand side, working from the other end.

The two inner corners of the gripping members will also have received a half dovetail cut. This will not affect subsequent passes with the router and the guides can be used many times over.

N.B. Trial cuts on scrap timber is essential, until the exact positions for the side fence has been obtained.

Tonguing and grooving

The making of tongued and grooved flooring is a simple operation when a router is combined with an arbor. A set of groovers with TCT cutting edges has now been designed specifically for use with all overhead routing machines and heavy duty hand routers, used portably or inverted as a 'mini-spindle'. These groovers are suitable for running at speeds of between 7,000 and 20,000 rpm. The tongue/groover set incorporates two four-winged TCT groovers and an arbor with adjustable spacers (see Fig. 37). The sets are available with arbors, having ⅜in. or ½in. diameter shanks. The tongue is

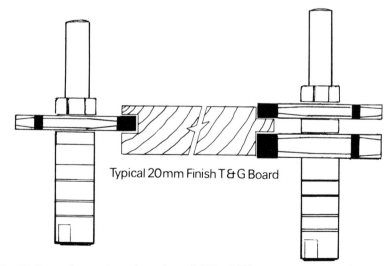

Typical 20mm Finish T & G Board

Fig.37. Cutters for tonguing and grooving: ref. 334 and 336.

produced by using the 6mm and 10mm groover in tandem. The groove to receive the tongue is made with the 6mm groover.

Making mortices

Mortices can be cut with a plunge router in several ways.

Portably, the router can groove mortice slots through a template (see chapter 4) or if workpiece is clamped in a bench vice with surface parallel with bench top, a slot can be cut most effectively. The full cutting depth should naturally be taken, say, ¼" at a time.

With router mounted overhead, a simple means of morticing is described in chapter 13.

The corners will at all times be radiused, but it is simpler to remove the corners of the tenons than chisel square the mortice corners.

Making tenons

With the router inverted and fitted beneath the table, small tenons can be cut cleanly and quickly using the sliding facility of the mitre fence (see Fig. 38.2). This fence is set at 90 deg. to the direction of cut. A sliding board is introduced to facilitate the forward movement when making the tenon. In operation, the batten to be tenoned is laid across the board with the end butting up against the adjustable side fence. It is held firmly against the mitre fence with the left hand.

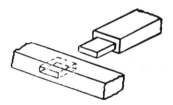

Fig.38. Diagram showing tenon and mortice joint. For making a mortice, refer to template construction (Chapter 5) or overhead routing (Chapter 13).

Fig.38.1. The finished tenon – clean and squarely cut.

Fig.38.2. Routing machine table with a sliding mitre fence.

Fig.38.3. The batten is rebated to form a tenon. The end of the cutter machines both sides squarely and cleanly. Note the support board, which ensures the workpiece is square to the fence.

The cutter used for this operation must have a 'bottom-cut' and is set to protrude vertically to the thickness of the tenon. It will be noted from Figs. 38.2 and 38.3 that the main fence is fitted with a flat strip; this is to allow the stub of the tenon to slide without hindrance. To cut the tenon, the mitre fence, sliding board and batten, are passed in the direction of the arrows, so that the batten end is trimmed by the cutter. The batten is then turned over to cut the opposite side and complete the tenon (Fig. 38.1).

Dowel drilling

Dowel jointing (see Figs. 39 and 39.2) is a useful means of jointing and can be carried out by the plunge drilling router. A simple jig is made for sinking dowel holes. Standard dowels are used for the tenons (dowel Ø = cutter Ø). The template jig used has equally spaced drilled

Fig.39. By making a simple drilling jig with holes to match the bush size on the router base, drilling holes for dowel joints is both fast and effective.

Fig.39.1. Exact matchings dowelled holes and pegs 8mm diameter, are ready for gluing. The drill jig with 17mm diam. holes to match 17mm O.D. bush, is seen in background.

Fig.39.2. An angular type clamp-on jig can be fitted over mitred corners to 'plunge' a series of apertures which will accept 8mm Ø dowels.

holes, 17mm Ø. These match the projecting guide bush diameter (17mm Ø O D) on the router base. If care has been taken to make the plywood jig, repetition jointing on a commercial scale is feasible. An angular type clamp-on jig can be fitted over mitred corners to 'plunge' a series of apertures to accept 8mm Ø dowels.

Mitre joints

Mitred corner joints are clean and attractive but often not very strong. However, a new introduction for the router, drawn from the cutting techniques used on spindle moulders, is a mitre jointing system. The procedure is based on using two 'rebating' cutters with 45° 'tail' sections, which mate together to form a 90° corner joint.

Whilst glueing together could be adequate for say, small cupboards and shelving, the usual procedure is to glue and screw strengthening blocks on the inside corners, which are usually hidden from view. See Fig. 39.3.

Fig.39.3. A mitre jointing system which can be adopted by those with min. 1200 watt routers to accept large router cutters seen at Figs 39.4 and 39.5. Note the reinforcement blocking, recommended for an extra strong mitred joint.

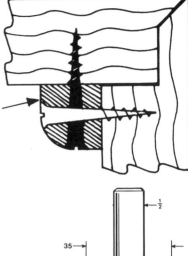

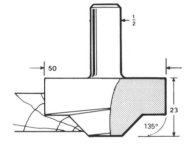

Fig.39.4. The 'Corner' groove mitre cutter ref. 84/80/12.

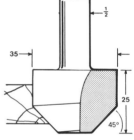

Fig.39.5. The 'Corner' tongue mitre cutter ref. 84/81/12.

9. Setting up for heavy duty applications

In this chapter we shall be portraying the heavier duty models MOF 31 and MOF 98, at 1,200 and 1,600 Watt input respectively. These will be of particular interest to those concerned with the heavy duty applications which are often encountered in the building trades.

Construction of heavy duty router

Figs. 40 and 40.1 show the basic construction of the router, which is fairly similar to its smaller counterpart, namely the Elu MOF 96. The main variations are the locking mechanism and the introduction of an adjustable height lock, which is completely independent of the depth lock bar (6). The depth locking lever is pressed to plunge the router down, and released to lock it in that position. Figs. 40 and 40.1 are self explanatory, most points having been discussed in the commentary on the smaller model in the range.

Setting to a given depth

Figs 40.2–40.5 describe the basic points for setting the router to reach to a given depth.

In this sequence, the routing depth A is portrayed as being sufficiently shallow to groove the work in one plunge. For example, a 16mm groove could be cut easily at 12 or 14mm depth, bearing in mind the power of the 1,600 Watt motor. However, when routing to greater depth, the rotary turret stop becomes invaluable.

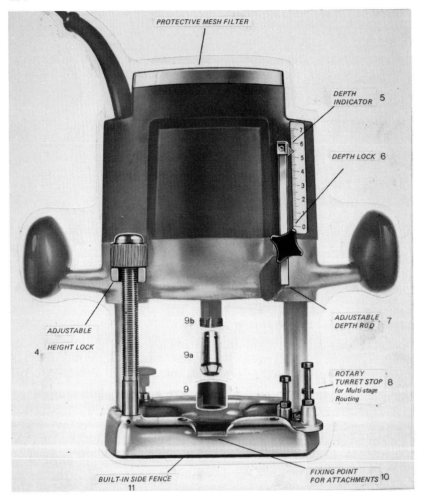

PROTECTIVE MESH FILTER

DEPTH INDICATOR 5

DEPTH LOCK 6

ADJUSTABLE DEPTH ROD 7

9b

ADJUSTABLE

HEIGHT LOCK

4

9a

9

ROTARY TURRET STOP 8 for Multi-stage Routing

BUILT-IN SIDE FENCE 11

FIXING POINT FOR ATTACHMENTS 10

Fig.40. The main features of 'plunger' router MOF 31 and 98. The depth setting system is clearly illustrated.

Fig.40.1. This plunge router has spring-loaded columns. Release of plunge lever locks the router in the depressed position.

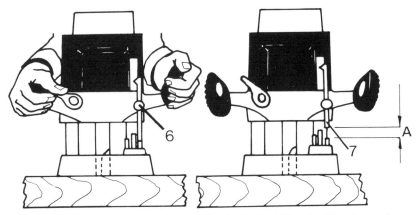

Fig.40.2. (Left) Loosen depth lock (6) and see that the depth rod (7) is free. Then depress plunge lever and carriage, so that the cutter rests on the workpiece. Now release lever so that router is locked down in that position.

Fig.40.3. (Right) Set the depth rod (7) so that the space between its base and the turret stop equals the depth of cut needed for the operation (A). Then tighten depth lock (6), depress lever to allow carriage to spring up.

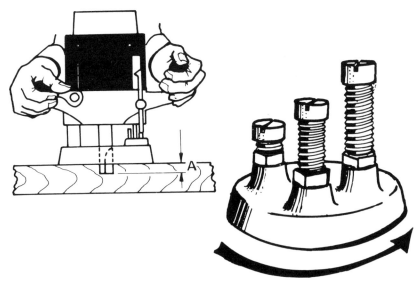

Fig.40.4. (Left) Switch on the motor, depress the lever and plunge router to the pre-set depth. Carry out the routing operation.

Fig.40.5. (Right) The set screws on the depth stop are in three lengths, but are themselves adjustable in height to provide the exact depth stop position to suit the operation.

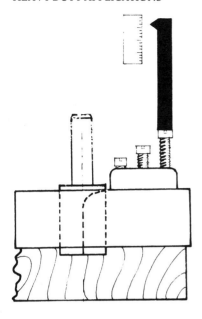

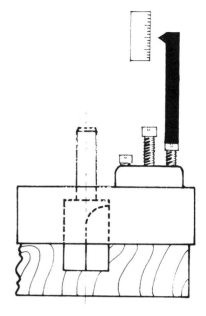

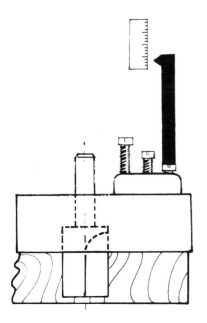

Fig.40.6. (Top left) Stage One, shallow cut. Depth bar locates on long threaded stop.

Fig.40.7. (Top right) Stage Two, second depth position reached. Depth bar locates on medium threaded stop.

Fig.40.8. (Left) Stage Three, third depth position reached. Depth bar locates on short threaded stop.

The rotary turret stop (Fig. 40.5)

In the previous paragraph we showed the method for setting the routing depth for a single plunge. However, more often than not the router is needed to perform at a greater depth than is advisable to work in one pass of the router. Therefore, we shall now show a typical multi-stage routing and cutting operation showing the use of the rotary turret stop. As can be seen from Figs. 40.6–40.8 the turret stops provide for three alternative depths of working. A ⅓ turn anti-clockwise if the turret head quickly offers a new depth with the depth rod engaging on the screw head.

Since changing from one depth to another is only a three-second operation, fast working is guaranteed and deep working can be undertaken without overloading the motor. The depth stop screws are in three lengths and when these are set to their required projection, back nuts are tightened to prevent them working loose.

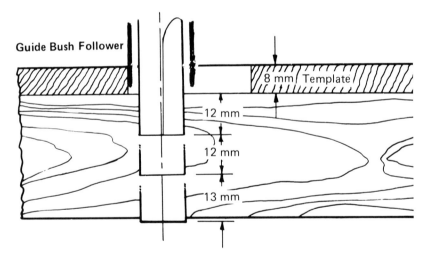

Fig.40.9. The 36mm thick door is to be cut in three stages as shown. Note the thickness of the template, which has to be allowed for when setting the depth of plunge.

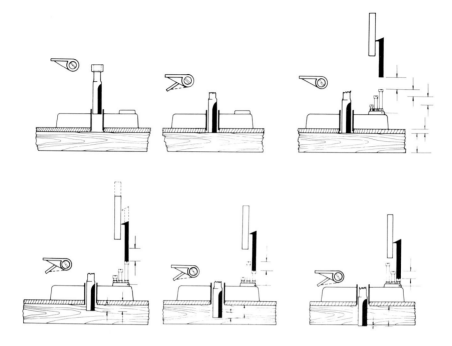

Fig.40.10. (Top left) A suitable cutter is chosen and fitted. In this case, a long-reach cutter, 37mm cut=depth, with diameter of 13mm.

Fig.40.11. (Top centre) Depress plunge lever and carriage so that cutter rests on workpiece, then release lever, to lock in that position.

Fig.40.12. (Top right) The workpiece is to be cut in three stages. 1. Set longest screw on turret depth stop to allow router to penetrate one-third of the workpiece, namely 12mm. 2. Set medium length screw to allow for cutting 12mm deep. 3. Set short screw to allow for cutting 13mm deep.

Fig.40.13. (Bottom left) Switch on motor. To make first cut, depress plunge lever and plunge cut the workpiece down to limit of long set screw. Rout groove guided by the template.

Fig.40.14. (Bottom centre) To make second cut, rotate anti-clockwise turret stop a ⅓ turn. Depress plunging lever and plunge cut to limit on medium screw and repeat routing operation as for the first cut.

Fig.40.15. (Bottom right) To make third cut, rotate turret stop anti-clockwise a ⅓ turn. Depress plunge lever and plunge cut to limit on short screw. The 13mm plunge will pierce the workpiece and allow the routed centre section to drop through. Depress lever, allowing carriage to spring up to original position (as at 40.10). Switch off motor.

Multi-stage cutting

The problem in hand is to rout an aperture in a solid door to provide a cut recess which is to be glazed. Figs. 40.10–40.15 describe graphically and in detail the procedure for routing out a clean-cut aperture to receive glazing beads. The method recommended includes the need for an 8mm thick template stuck, clamped or pinned to the door face (see Fig. 40.9). (Template design and construction is dealt with in Chapter 5.)

10. Drilling with the router

The very real advantages of being able to drill with a router, have not 'come home' to the average woodworker. In fact the idea of drilling with any tool other than a hand drill or pillar drill could be thought of as a form of heresy! Drilling with a router should, however, only be attempted with a plunging type hand router, which has spring-loaded columns, e.g. the Elu.

The 'plunging' facility in the router creates a number of useful applications which are not available with the conventional router. For example, suitable cutters can produce pre-drilled holes to accept screws and bolts. The holes are clean-cut and parallel and of a far superior quality to the conventionally drilled ones. The secret is the high cutting speed. If the cutter is sharp a fine clean cut, almost polished, is obtained. A word of advice is needed here, however, for it is not advisable to attempt such work in any direction other than downwards. The reason is that it is difficult to obtain a good purchase on the router to plunge the carriage horizontally or in an upwards direction. The plunge drilling router can also provide a useful means of dowel jointing.

Plunge type cutters

We should mention the importance of cutters used for drilling pur-poses. These have cutting edges on their bases and, as in the engineering trades, are often termed 'end mill' cutters. With the advent of the plunging router, however, the term 'plunge cut' has been adopted.

The router bit for drilling purposes should ideally have clearance of approximately 20 deg. (ground back from the leading edge). While HSS cutters are usually ground to give a good clearance, small cutters of ¼in. and below are not easy to grind in this way. Solid TC cutters on the other hand present no difficulties in obtaining good relief. These are now often chosen if clean-cut small holes without burn marks are especially required. With this type of cutter it is possible to enter the work from above as well as from the edge. The router motor must necessarily be brought down into the work through the action of a foot pedal in a fixed-head router (such as the Trend), or by manual pressure in a portable 'plunging' router (such as the Elu).

Drilling speeds

The success of drilling with the router is based on the fast clean cutting action, with quick chip clearance.

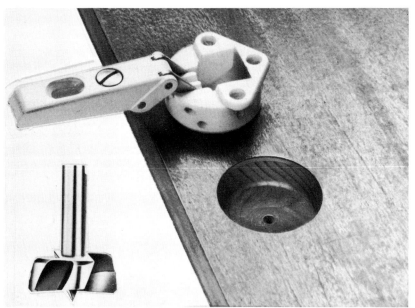

Fig.41. By using a Trend Hinge Sinking Cutter Type 421, a most practical method of cutting clean holes to receive circular hinges is obtained.
N.B. *These sinking cutters should only be used with plunging type routers, overhead routers or pillar drills.*

Cutters above 25mm diameter may need to be plunged in stages of 12mm at one time, as the high speed of the router has self-defeated the original advantage. Variable speed routers offer the facility of bringing the speed down to nearer 10,000 rpm, which is more appropriate for large drilling cutters such as the Hinge Sinkers described in Fig. 41).

Plug and knot-hole borers (see Fig. 42)

The removal of an unsightly knots or screw holes in plywood or timber can be carried out most efficiently if a matching pair of plug and hole makers are chosen. These cutters are designed in such a way that a perfect tight fit can be guaranteed. The plug will need a light tape to fit into position.

Hinge sinking cutters

Round hinges, particularly in the furniture industry, are very much in common use now, the main advantage being the simplicity with which

Fig.42. Removing of unsightly knots and covering of drilled or counterbored holes can be done with the plunge router, if special matching tools are used.

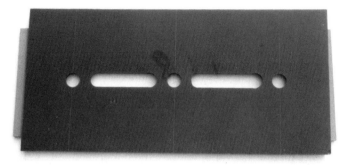

Fig.43. This template, made from 6mm thick perspex was clamped over the leg illustrated below. The 17mm Ø bush on the router base located in the aperture. With a 12/3 10mm diam. radius cutter fitted, only a 3mm plunge depth was needed to provide the attractive indentation effect.

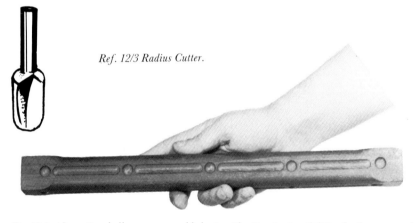

Ref. 12/3 Radius Cutter.

Fig.43.1. Alternative shallow grooves and holes provide attractive possibilities for those engaged in decorative work. Cutter used was a Ref. 12/7 radius cutter.

they can be fixed (see Fig. 41). A special range of hinge sinking cutters is available now for use with 'plunging' routers.

Decorative work

The possibilities for decorative applications are unlimited. Cutters with 'bottom cut' facilities will produce dimples and shaped indentations with attractive results. Combinations of dimples and grooves (as

Fig.44. The router is inverted to show how an acrylic 'see-through' plate with cross datum lines can be fixed to the router base.

illustrated in Fig. 43.1) on chair legs, lamp standards and so on, present a great challenge to one's creative abilities.

Useful hints for drilling by hand

Feedback of information from the trade, prompts me to mention a few simple but invaluable innovations. First, it is worth mentioning a simple means of ensuring that the router remains still when the carriage is plunged down. If both base and workpiece are slippery a slight movement when plunging will cause an oval hole to be drilled.

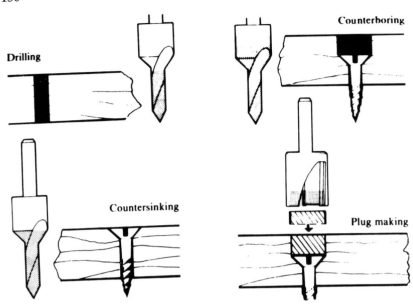

Fig.45. (Top left) Drilling tool, ref 62, is drilling a square clean-cut hole.

Fig.45.1. (bottom left) The same tool, brought down further into the work, has produced a countersink.

Fig.45.2. (Top right) The same drill taken further still, has produced a counterbored hole.

Fig.45.3. (Bottom right) A plug-making cutter, ref 24, will produce a plug to cover up a counterbored hole. A light press fit produces a first-class joint.

Fig.45.4. This Elu routing jig incorporates a plunging head, with vertical and lateral movement, and variable stops. It will drill key holes, lock handle shafts and, when swung over, it will rout a shallow recess for the lock plate.

The solution is to fit a sheet of fine sanding paper to the router base, using double-sided adhesive tape. It's as simple as that!

One minor criticism of drilling with a router is the sighting of the position where the hole is to be drilled. However, the following procedure overcomes this set-back. A 'false' base, made from a clear acrylic sheet, is secured to the router base (with standard fixing screws or double-sided tape). A single plunge drilled hole locates the centre point of the cross, then datum lines are engraved on the outer face and filled with black enamel. The sighting of pre-marked drilling points is now a quick and simple operation (see Fig. 44).

Drilling, countersinking, counterboring and plugging (see Figs. 45–45.3)

There is now a one-piece tungsten tipped drilling tool available for use with the 'plunging' router which has a triple application. It can be used in either plunging routers or power drills. It is available in three sizes to suit No. 8, 10, and 12 wood screws. Not only will it drill holes, but if brought further down into the workpiece, will countersink them also. Bringing the tool down still deeper gives clean cut apertures or counterbores. The apertures are so accurate and square that cover plugs can be fitted most effectively. (Ref. group 24 range of plug cutters shown in Chapter 17, are suitable for this purpose.)

Drilling key holes in wood doors

Devices for drilling holes for ironmongery provide just one more application of the totally underrated router system which is used for making apertures. The clever appliance shown in Fig. 45.4, clamps onto the door edge for drilling key and door handle shafts. When swung over, it will recess a groove to receive the lock plate.

Drilling jig device – see Fig. 46

This home-made drilling jig was made from scrap material and offcuts. It enables two pairs of holes to be drilled or countersunk, with considerable speed and to exact present positions.

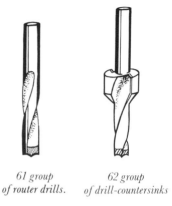

61 group
of router drills.

62 group
of drill-countersinks

Fig.45.5.

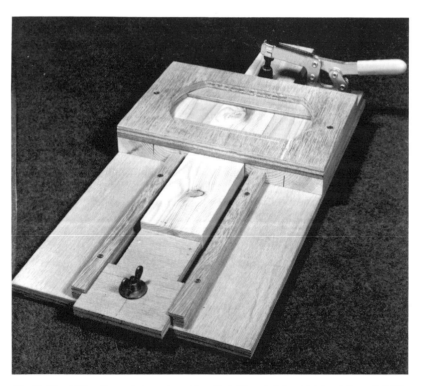

Fig.46. The drilling jig, end view, shows the adjustable end stop, which is set for each drilling position. This home-made jig forms the basis for other jigs when batch or mass production is envisaged.

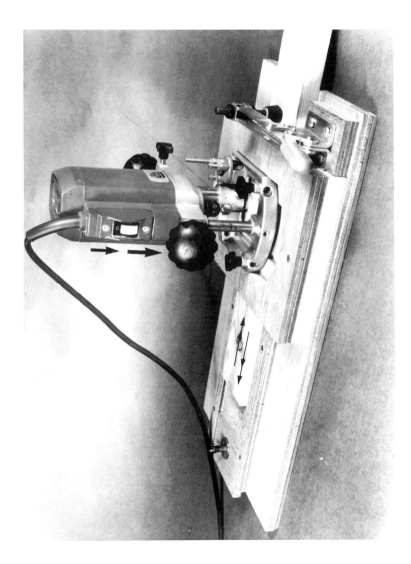

Fig.46.1. The drilling jig, side view, shows the router mounted ready for the first plunge.

Fig.47. A pair of clean cut 90 deg. holes plunge-drilled with the router using a Ref. 61/10 TCT router drill.

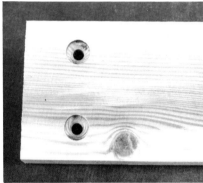

Fig.47.1. A pair of drilled and countersunk holes. The router gives an almost polished finish with the plung action ensuring a 90 deg. square entry. A one-piece combination drill/countersink Ref. 62/10 was used.

The principle of the jig is based on two running tracks. The router slides within a 'shoe' to two different positions, and the workpiece slides at right angles, to it. A toggle clamp holds it down when it has reached the limit stop.

Those who have carried out drilling operations with a router will vouch for the clean and almost polished finish obtained. Furthermore the plunge action ensures a 90 deg. entry.

The Router drills, which have special fluting and lip and spur TC tips, are shown at Fig. 45.5. The one-piece drill/countersink illustrated will drill and countersink in one operation.

11. Use of arbors for grooving and cutting

It would be true to say that the router is the most under-rated tool in the woodworking trade. Those who possess them rarely use them to their full potential and so in this chapter we shall look at a whole range of applications and show just how versatile the hand router can be. Some very useful machining applications can be found by fitting the router with arbors instead of cutters. They will accept groovers, slitting blades, trimmers and saw blades and are available in two basic types: the light duty ones (see Figs. 48, 48.1 and 48.2) which are designed for such jobs as edge slotting, trimming, recessing for weather strip inserts, and a recent application, slitting double glazed units for reclaiming glass; and heavy duty ones which are used for such work as tongueing and grooving, or trimming off flash in the plastics industry. The component parts of the heavy duty arbor, and its various groovers, slotters and blades are shown in Fig. 49.3. An interesting innovation is the undercut groover for introducing a plastic liner or weatherproof strip (see Figs. 48.3 and 48.4).

These arbors can also be used when the router is mounted beneath the work table (as a mini-spindle, see Chapter 12). In this instance the material is fed into the cutting head and providing safety guards are utilised to conform to health and safety regulations, a full range of new applications is opened up.

Undercut Grooving

Often in builder's joinery, a draught excluder slot needs to be inserted sometimes, even after frames have been assembled. A groove or

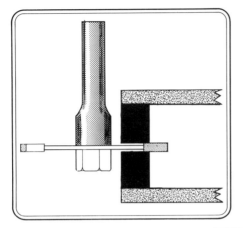

Fig.48. Slitting the mastic jointing of a double glazed sealed unit: a narrow necked arbor is used with a TC slitting blade.

Fig.48.1. Trimming the plastic overlay and simultaneously slotting the edge for insertions of barbed edge strip. Ref 47/1 90° trimmer. TC has slotter SL/E, fitted to its base to give a 'key' for accepting an edge strip.

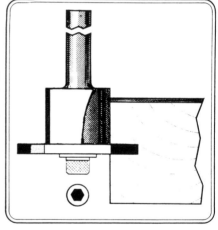

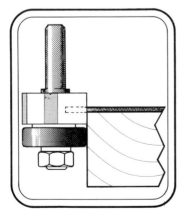

Fig.48.2. The arbor 33/6 has been fitted with a 3 fluted TC trimmer ref. 34/6, also B16 bearing for guidance purposes, thus avoiding the need for a side fence guide.

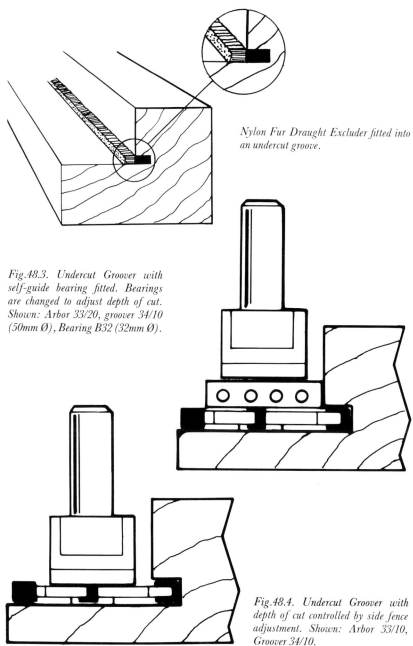

Nylon Fur Draught Excluder fitted into an undercut groove.

Fig.48.3. Undercut Groover with self-guide bearing fitted. Bearings are changed to adjust depth of cut. Shown: Arbor 33/20, groover 34/10 (50mm Ø), Bearing B32 (32mm Ø).

Fig.48.4. Undercut Groover with depth of cut controlled by side fence adjustment. Shown: Arbor 33/10, Groover 34/10.

Fig.48.5. (Right) Undercut groover, when removed from arbor, shows the threaded portion: groover ref. is 34/12.

narrow slot may be needed in the base and corner of the rebate. The groovers offered for this work, thread on to the arbors, and can therefore cut flush with the workpiece.

Two types are offered – Arbor 33/10 accepts the groove only, whilst the longer one, 33/20, accepts interchangeable guide bearings. With the latter, a router can be used without a side fence, as the bearing engages the wall of the rebated section. To choose bearings for required cutting depth, a chart is available – see Chapter 17.

Recessing draught excluder strip

There are a number of such products on the general market, but most are unsightly or impermanent. To fit such a weather strip profession-ally is now within the scope of the amateur. An example is given below of a brush strip with a 'keyed' or 'barbed' insertion edge (see Fig. 49). The arbor type 33/9 is fitted with a slotter in the ref. 47/7A-D range, which is bolted to the base of the arbor. A slotter which can cut between 1.5mm and 3mm wide can cope with most recessing work of this nature. If the depth of the router is adjusted up or down, the width of slot can be widened to suit the occasion. (In certain instances the

Fig.49. Slide in the draught excluder strip.

brush strip housing may need to be recessed too.) Depth of groove can be adjustable by fitting bearings of various diameters.

Reclaiming double glazed units

Owing to the high cost of glass it has now been found to be economical to reclaim damaged units (see Fig. 49.2). The Elu power trimmer has

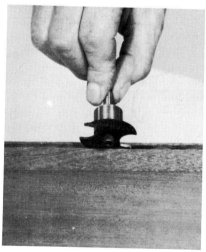

Fig.49.1. Narrow slot to receive draught excluder.

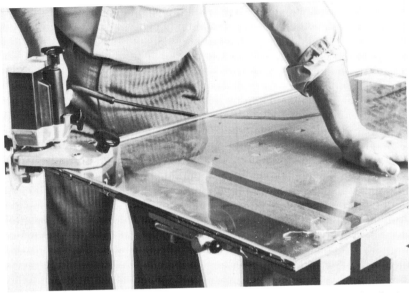

Fig.49.2. Reclaiming glass; an Elu power trimmer type 67 is used to slit double-glazed units. This machine can slit a unit 4 ft square in less than 2 minutes. Thin wedges are fitted behind the tool at approximately 1 ft intervals.

been especially adapted to split the sides of double glazed units in order that the glass can be salvaged and re-used. In fact, most small routers can be used for this purpose, but a false base should be fitted to counterbalance the machine to prevent it tipping and shattering the glass.

Heavy duty arbors

Arbors and the tooling used with heavy duty hand routers, namely those above 1½ hp, present a valuable asset on the building site. So often, unforseen machining work becomes necessary, particularly when the joinery shop has a full quota of work. The machine table, which fits into the back of a car boot, can be erected in minutes, and set up to perform such jobs as grooving, rebating, and trimming. The arbor assembly (see Fig. 49.3) with its various groovers and blades, together with an optional roller bearing for guidance, offers plenty of scope for such operations.

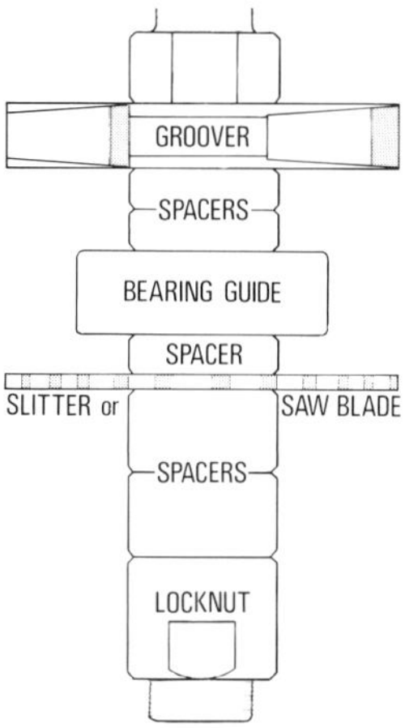

(Left) The arbor assembly diagram shows the make-up of the components. Shank is available in ³⁄₈ and ¹⁄₂ diam. only.

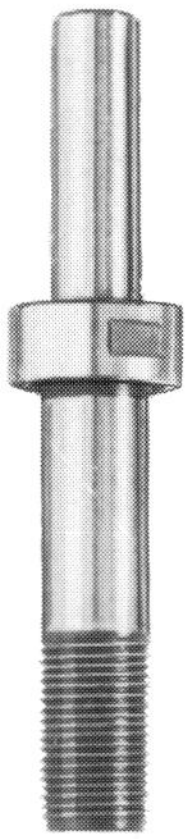

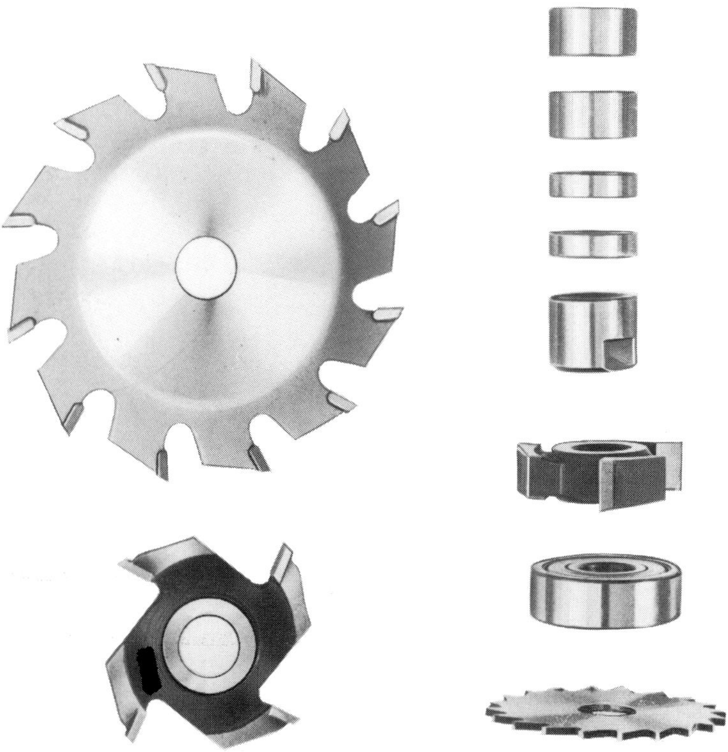

GROOVER

SPACERS

BEARING GUIDE

SPACER

SLITTER or SAW BLADE

SPACERS

LOCKNUT

Fig.49.3. This heavy duty arbor in 'expoded' view is shown with various groovers, slotters, and blades. The bearing shown can be used as a guide running against the board edge.

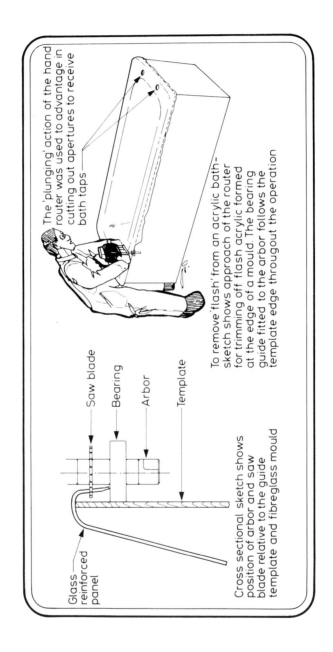

The 'plunging' action of the hand router was used to advantage in cutting out apertures to receive bath taps

To remove 'flash' from an acrylic bath-sketch shows approach of the router for trimming off flash acrylic formed at the edge of a mould The bearing guide fitted to the arbor follows the template edge througout the operation

Saw blade

Bearing

Arbor

Template

Glass reinforced panel

Cross sectional sketch shows position of arbor and saw blade relative to the guide template and fibreglass mould

Fig. 49.4. Trimming off 'flash' from acrylic bath tops.

Trimming off 'flash'

A router is the ideal powered tool for trimming off the edges of 'flash' as it is called in the trade. There are a number of ways in which the router can be applied in conjunction with a template, but Fig. 49.4 shows a system for trimming acrylic bath tops. A template can be fitted over the top of the bath or, as shown in the illustration, on the vertical plane.

A protective sheet of material (not shown) is needed to protect the bath edge from being scratched by the base of the router. There is a definite advantage in a 'plunging' router for this work, because the taps, overflow and waste can all be routed out with the same machine using a cutter of the 421 group, see Chapter 17.

12. The router as a fixed machine

Machining work as a whole, is not carried out on the building site, but back in the joinery shop. However, with a light-duty machining table, better described as a light-duty spindle, there are a number of jobs which can be done on the building site. A few of the applications are as follows: production of mouldings for architraves and skirtings, short runs of tongueing and grooving, rebating, tenoning (see Chapter 8 for all), trimming formica edges, edge slotting for draught excluders . . . the list continues indefinitely.

Naturally, we are talking about relatively short runs of work, but how invaluable to be able to carry out such applications on the spot! So often the building specification is subject to modifications and the client requires extras not originally allowed for in the joinery shop.

The equipment one requires consists basically of an inverted hand router (Elu in this instance) fitted into a special table which, while small, is stable and provides a solid working surface. As will be seen from Fig. 50, provision is made for an adjustable side fence with spring loaded clamps (Fig. 51) to hold the material firm when machining.

These clamps hold the material down while it is being fed in and also constitute protection guards, and as such, are looked on favourably by the Health and Safety authorities. All this equipment can be purchased complete for between £200 and £250, depending on the accessories required. One attraction is that of portability, as it can be taken from site to site in the back of a small van. It is available in 110V and 230V (single phase) to comply with local electricity supply regulations.

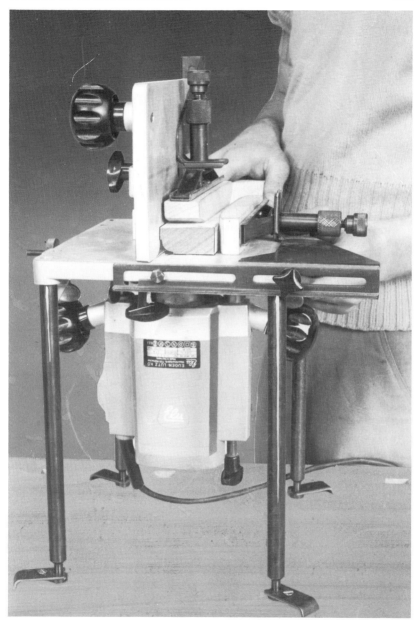

Fig.50. This router machine table is ideal for short runs of machining work. The spring-loaded clamps hold the work steady and act as protection guards.

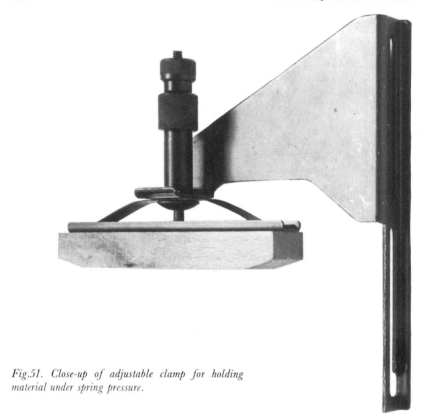

Fig.51. Close-up of adjustable clamp for holding material under spring pressure.

Copy profiling on the machine table

By using doublesided tape to secure the workpiece to the template, see Fig. 52 (a ceramic tile) simple and effective copy profiling was undertaken.

A self-guide cutter, with roller bearing mounted on its shank, was used with the router fitted in a machine router table.

Cutters ref. 46/90 or 46/10 are recommended for these operations. Note that workpiece is applied clockwise against the cutter, (opposite to that when router is used manually).

Fig.52. (Right) Attractive shaped plaques or cutting boards can be profiled from a master template. (Bottom) The workpiece which has been rough bandsawed prior to affixing to template, is seen being profiled on a routing table. (Below) Special self-guide cutter, ideally suited for copy-profile applications described, cutter Ref. 46/10 (guard removed for clarity).

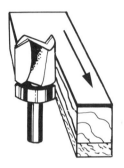

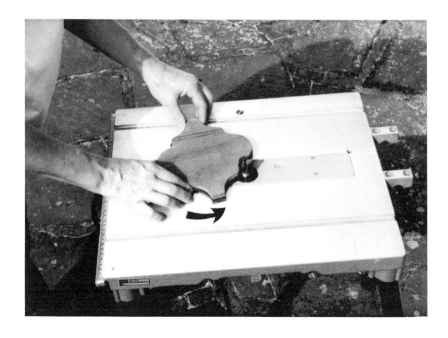

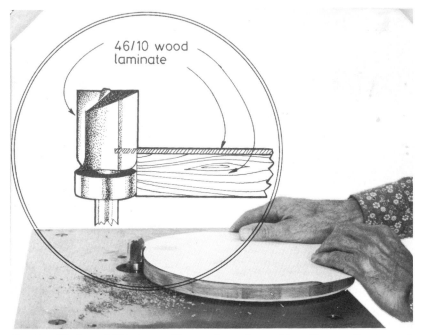

Fig.52.1. The latest 46/10 trimmer. The use of a routing machine table comes 'into its own', when trimming of laminate edges on a curved workpiece is involved.

Direction of feed

Always feed the material in the opposite direction to that in which the cutter is rotating. Remember that when the cutter is projecting upwards the direction of cut is opposite to that when the cutter is pointing downwards (i.e. when hand routing).

Machine table with guide roller

For profiling shaped workpieces, such as a plywood cot, see Fig. 52.1, a shaped template is secured to the plywood panels by nails or double sided tape. The template engages on an overhead mounted roller with the cutter fitted to the inserted router immediately below, trimming the plywood to the pattern. If the straight cutter is replaced by a radiused one, a moulded edge can replace the square one (see Fig. 52.2).

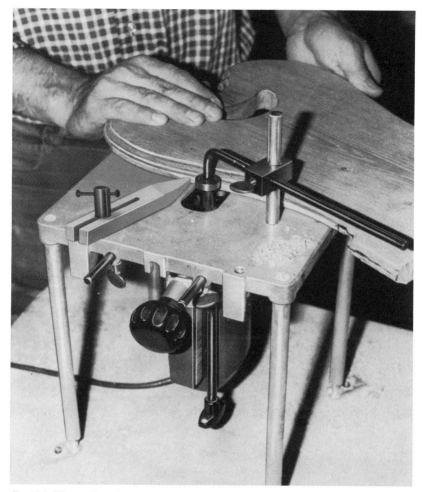

Fig.52.2. The small machine table as set up for profiling a child's cot end. A template, secured to the workpiece with double-sided tape, runs against a roller bearing follower mounted over the cutter. Exact alignment is necessary and the table mounting must be carefully secured.

Rebating on the machine table

Fig. 53.1 shows once again how the machine table can be firmly fixed in to a carpenter's bench, and in this instance, used to rebate a grand-father clock face over the projecting cutter. The fine adjustment facility on the router is used to obtain the exact depth of cut.

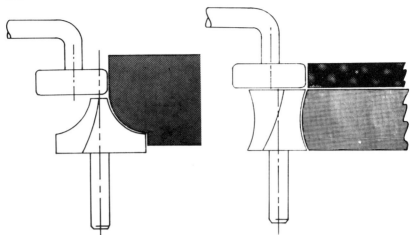

Fig.52.3. and 52.4. The independent overhead bearing system on a small router table, which emphasizes the positions required so that the workpiece can follow the board edge (52.3. left) or template edge (52.4. right). Standard two flute cutters are used as these have bottom-cut clearance. See Appendix.

Angular machine table

One accessory for the MOF 96 router is an angular machine table which clamps to the edge of the workshop table. The cutter protrudes horizontally (see Fig. 53.1) and the side of the cutter removes the material.

Fig. 53 shows a small window frame being rebated along its outer edges. Once more, the spring loaded clamp serves dual purpose roles.

Small mini-spindle

A small machine table, powered by a router, can be most productive. For instance, making one's own mouldings from square battening presents a very real economy in these times of high timber costs. When working narrow material for making, say, window sash bars or picture frame mouldings, a 'suva' clamp (Fig. 51) can be fitted to the horizontal fence plate, and a second one will ensure that the material being machined is held firmly against the cutter in both directions (see Fig. 50).

An even finish throughout the length of the workpiece can thus be

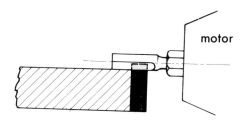

motor

Fig.52.4. A 3/50 10mm Ø cutter fitted laterally to the router.

obtained. This can be an important factor when making up frames with mitred corners. The additional safety measures the clamps provide should be mentioned, they both protect the operator from the exposed cutter and conform to safety regulations.

Fig.53. With the machine table mounted laterally on the workbench, further possibilities are opened up. Here a window is being rebated on all sides.

Fig.53.1. The small machine table which is supplied as an accessory with Elu MOF 96 router, is seen fitted to a carpenter's workbench. The strong 'T' shaped base panel enables the machine table to be clamped quickly into the vice of the workbench.

Fig.53.2. A double ovollo mould was cut on the table illustrated on the left. Cutter Ref. 7/4 was used.

A small router table

The machine table is seen in Fig. 53 fitted to a simple wood base, which in turn fits into a carpenters' bench and is secured firmly in place. A home-made side fence has been fitted, and a compound moulded edge is obtained by passing the material over the projecting cutter. A fine screw feed depth adjuster is rotated in a clockwise or anti-clockwise direction to bring the cutter up or down as required. The cutter used to obtain the mould effect was ref. 7/6 (see Chapter 17), set at varying depths.

Fig.53.4. The system for trimming hardwood lipping is clearly shown when the pressure clamp is removed to expose the side of the cutter.

Trimming hardwood lipping

The same set-up as for rebating can be used for trimming hardwood lipping. Fig. 53.4 illustrates this clearly. The spring 'suva' clamp has been omitted to give a clearer view of the cutter in relation to the hardwood edging.

Shaping letters (see Fig. 53.5)

Some sign makers prefer to use an inverted router, as opposed to an overhead one. The illustration shows a letter 'E' being bevelled. The cutters used for this purpose have a guide pin fitted to their base (Fig. 53.6). They are ideal for profiling materials which have small intricate shapes, as the guide pin is able to reach right into the corners.

Fig.53.5. Cutting out of letters and components can be undertaken on the router table. The use of chamfer cutters with guide pins to finish the edges is now standard practice by sign makers. The illustration shows a 40 deg. chamfer being put on an acrylic letter E.

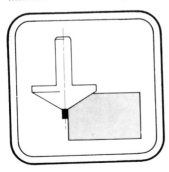

Fig.53.6. A chamfer cutter, type 10F, has a guide pin mounted on its base for following the edge.

Larger machine table (Fig. 54)

So far in this chapter on routing tables, we have shown how even small routers (below 1000 watts) can be fitted in reverse position and used effectively to machine small components.

The larger routing table now described will accept routers up to 2000 watts. Dust extraction is an optional extra (see Fig. 54.1), together with spring loaded pressure pads, which act as protection guards, thus complying with safety regulations.

The facility for a sliding mitre fence is invaluable. E.g. making tenons and machining the ends of transoms, mullions, etc. (Ref. Chapter 8).

Fig.54. This table approx. 2'6"×1'6" is shown with adjustable side fence and hold down clamps which act as protection guards as well as means for keeping workpiece under pressure whilst feeding in.

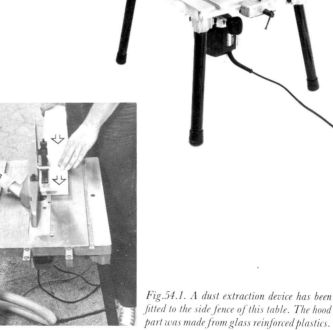

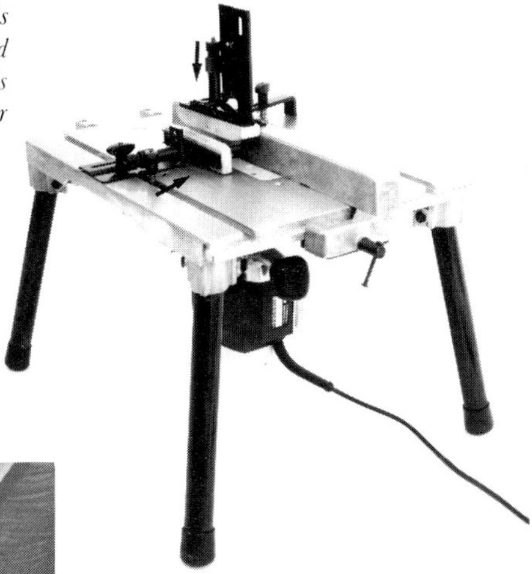

Fig.54.1. A dust extraction device has been fitted to the side fence of this table. The hood part was made from glass reinforced plastics.

Fig.54.2. The machine table is fitted with a sliding fence for the scribing operation when a reverse mould and groove is cut simultaneously across the grain. Cutter set used was a SAS/4. Note the adjustable pressure guard, raised for clarity.

Fig.54.3. Side fence with mitre facility is set at 90°.

Fig.54.4. Close up showing the tenon and scribed mould which was cut simultaneously.

Fig.54.5. With router mounted in inverted position, the machine table is set up to profile the mould and groove simultaneously along the grain. Cutter set fitted was a PAS/4. Refer to scriber set which exactly matches it.

Fig.54.6. Close-up view showing the classic mould and groove which was cut simultaneously (guard removed for clarity).

Home-made table

The cost of a factory made routing table is around the £100 mark, with D.I.Y. quality ones being very much cheaper, but not substantial enough for the majority of industrial routers. A home-made router table can be constructed quite simply from ¾in blockboard or preferably two layers of ½in thick plywood. Figs 57.3–57.5.

A side fence will be needed and this should be slotted to adjust the fence laterally as necessary.

Home-made fine adjuster.

For those who intend to machine edges of boards, a fine adjustment device can be built into the side fence. The author built this to his own design, and details of construction are shown in Fig. 57.2.

Machining profiles and scribes

The latest profile/scriber sets are designed for use with all heavy duty routers with 1,200–2,000 watts power factor, they are only recommended for fitting into ⅜in or ½in collets.

Each set comprises of an arbor each fitted with a T.C. mould cutter, groover and self guide bearing. The matching scriber sets provide exact fitting joints for transoms, mullions, or decorative panelling. Such operations are normally carried out on a spindle moulder but miniaturisation of tools now provide for this work to be performed with any heavy duty router.

It opens up new horizons for those possessing this versatile power tool, especially if they are prepared to invest in a router machine table. An invaluable accessory.

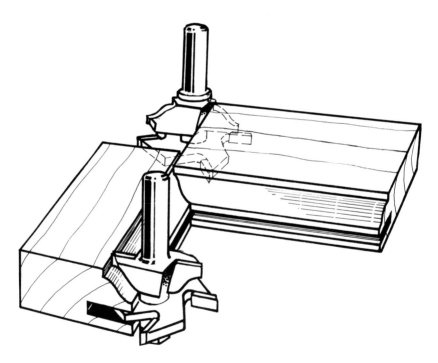

Fig.55. Illustration shows a classic profile set with machining scriber counterpart.

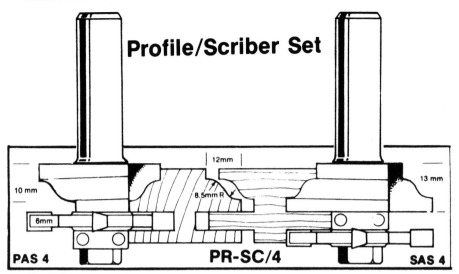

Profile/Scriber Set

Fig.55.1.

Operational notes

These tools are made for use with fixed head routers or heavy duty hand routers of 650 watts rating and above, preferably mounted in machine tables.

They are designed for collets (chucks) with capacity of 8mm (⁵⁄₁₆in), ³⁄₈in and ¹⁄₂in. Arbors with ¹⁄₄in shanks should only be mounted with *one* groove or *one* mould cutter at one time.

Should a 4mm tongue and groove be preferred to the 6mm one which is standard, they can be supplied to special order.

When hand routers are used, it has been found more satisfactory to

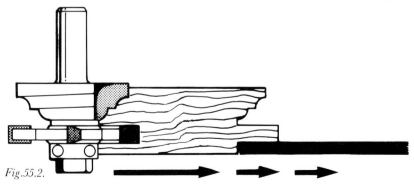

Fig.55.2.

set the router up on a machine table. It provides better support and guidance facilities. However, should the machining work be carried out portably, the following should be observed. Having machined across the grain using the SAS set, an extension strip of min. 6mm thick material should be glued or clamped to the table at the end of the workpiece, so as to form a 'run-off' board. This offers a bearing surface on which the guide roller can follow. (It prevents the bearing on the PAS set running into the groove cut by the scriber set.)

Prefabricated routing fixtures

A range of components are now commercially available which enables the router to be mounted vertically above or below a table top. See Figs 56 and 56.1.

It also allows the router to traverse along slide bars. See Fig. 56.

The square M. Steel blocks, not only act as structural connectors, but can be utilised as limit stops, and securing points for the working top when router is fitted below in spindle position.

Fig.56. The modular system shown above, lends itself to machine table routing. A table top can be secured to the blocks which have M6 threaded holes.

Fig.56.1. Router mounted overhead allows material to be passed beneath it for grooving operation.

Fig.56.2. Router is mounted from beneath, using same components. An edge moulding operation is being undertaken with a self-guide cutter, ref. 46/23.

Fig.56.3. Router is mounted in a prefabricated stand. Note the adjustable stops.

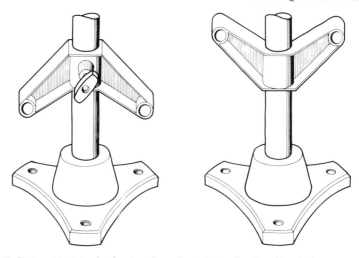

Fig.57. Basic support stands, showing alternative positions for winged bracketing.

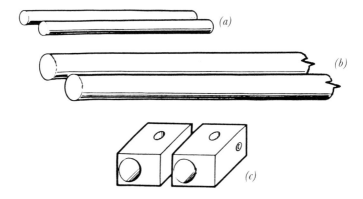

Fig.57.1. (a) Small guide rods 8mm diameter 300mm long. (c) Larger guide rods, 18mm diameter. These are available in different lengths. (c) Connecting blocks with 8mm and 18mm apertures, with grub securing screws (M6).

Home-made routing tables

There are those who prefer to make their own tables, and if they have the time and patience, can introduce features which will give more potential and accuracy than the bought-in one.

The table should be rigidly made to withstand vibration. Preferably, the top should be made of two 10mm thick plywood sheets, alternatively blockboard or chipboard. Fig. 57.3 shows a free-standing one. 57.4 shows a folding one, for those with a space problem. One end clamps onto the work bench. The hinged end should have support struts also hinged.

As the router's depth capacity can be severely limited by the worktop, a central plate approx. 9in square, made from $^{3}/_{16}$in or $^{1}/_{4}$in steel should be inserted, complete with 'pick-up' points for bolting it on the router base.

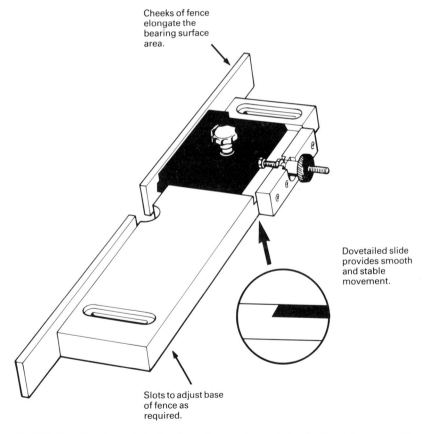

Cheeks of fence
elongate the
bearing surface
area.

Dovetailed slide
provides smooth
and stable
movement.

Slots to adjust base
of fence as
required.

Fig.57.2. Drawing shows the basic points of interest. In particular the Fine Adjustment of the slide and lock knob to secure.

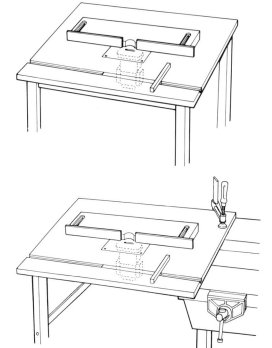

Fig.57.3. Home made free-standing table.

Fig.57.4. Home made fold-up table for clamping on work bench.

Fig.57.5. Sliding cross fence is invaluable for such work as tenoning and scribing.

Adjustable fence

If a fence is made on the lines designed by the author, it will surely be superior to the 'standard' commercial one. The fence should have the end part adjustable, so that when machining the edges, the fence can project out and compensate for the part removed by the router. Fig. 57.6 shows the suggested design, which preferably should incorporate a dovetail slide.

Extension pieces can be stuck (double sided tape) to the two fence sections, when extra bearing surface is required. A fine adjustment of

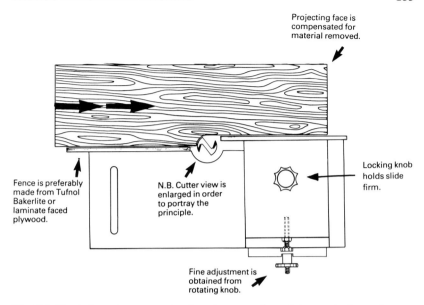

Projecting face is
compensated for
material removed.

Locking knob
holds slide
firm.

Fence is preferably
made from Tufnol
Bakerlite or
laminate faced
plywood.

N.B. Cutter view is
enlarged in order
to portray the
principle.

Fine adjustment is
obtained from
rotating knob.

Fig.57.6. Sketch shows the compensating factor in respect of material removed after machining.

the slide is helpful, though not essential, but a locking knob or bolt to secure it firmly is necessary.

Sliding fence

For tenoning, scribing, and trimming, a sliding fence to run at 90° to the fence (if fence needed), is quite invaluable.

Once more, if this can be dovetailed to slide into the work top, so much the better, for accuracy and stability.

Dust extraction

A modified vacuum cleaner hood fitting can be mounted on the fence body to extract most of the chips, should dust present a problem.

Fig.57.8. A further example of how standard cutters can be given a self-guiding feature. Classic cutter ref. 20/30 has been fitted with a ½" diam. roller bearing on its shank.

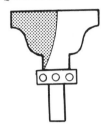

Fig.57.9. Edge moulding is obtained by spinning the workpiece against a scribing mould cutter. This has a ½" diam. roller bearing mounted on its shank. For this operation, the bearing follows the base edge of the plaque. Black arrow points to 'anti-kick' block, stuck down on table top with double sided tape. This assists the guidance of the workpiece when engaging the cutter.

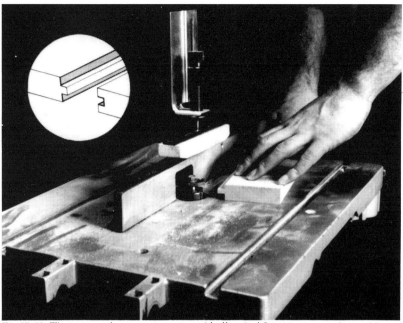

Fig.57.10. The tongue and groove cutters sets are ideally suited for routers mounted in a table, note the pressure guard has been raised for clarity.

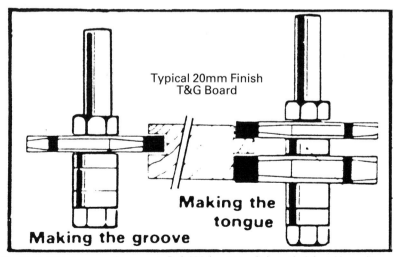

Fig.57.11. This tongue and groove set, Ref. 336 (see Appendix), is ideal for table machine use. With the one arbor and two T.C. groovers, the T and G application can be performed with routers of 1,200 Watt rating and above.

13. Overhead routing applications

There are numerous pros and cons for portable routers as against fixed head routers, but if copy routing is involved, that is reproducing a number of components from a master pattern, for example, wood platters, table mets, shaped trays, the outlay for buying a fixed head router could be justified. The cost could well be 4–6 times that of a hand router.

The expression 'fixed head' is rather misleading for in operation, the router head slides down at 90 deg. to engage the workpiece from despression of a foot pedal, or hand lever. The advantages of the foot pedal versus the manual approach will speak for itself, but once done, it is the question of weighing up the cost with the benefits.

We shall now describe some typical applications.

Copy routing

The copy routing system is based on reproducing articles from a master template which is affixed to the base of the workpiece. The template engages on a guide pin projecting up from the centre of the worktable. The pin aligns exactly with the cutter above. By adjusting the cutter size, type and depth; also the guide pin diameter, variations from the original pattern are obtained. However, to produce an exact replica of the template, the cutter must match the pin. E.g. 6mm diam. pin requires a 6mm router bit (1 : 1 ratio).

In operation, the foot pedal is depressed which brings the router head down to engage the cutter into the workpiece. An adjustable depth stop working on the same principle as the turret stop on most modern hand routers, determines the depth of plunge. Once the

Fig.58. Overhead routing with a router fitted into a factory made machine stand (guard has been removed for clarity).

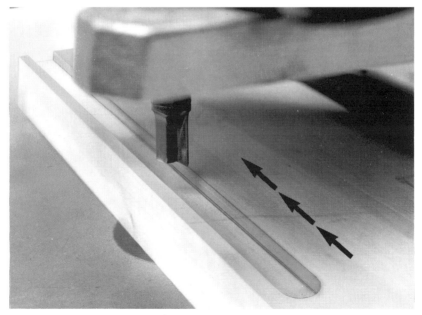

Fig.58.1. Clear vision for working is one attractive feature when machining on an overhead machine router.

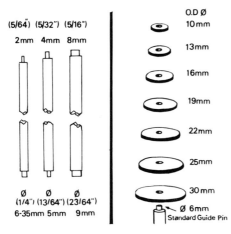

Fig.58.2. A range of guide pins and bushes offer a number of cutting variations without changing the template.

router head has reached its full stroke, a hand lever is flicked over to lock it in that position. The operator's hands are now free to manipulate the workpiece over the guide pin, and cut or profile as required. When machining is complete, release of the hand lock allows the router head to spring back up to original position. A point to remember, if you are profiling, that is cutting on the edge of the workpiece, move it in a clockwise direction, i.e. against the rotation of

Fig.58.3. The guide pin, which engages into the template base, is adjustable in height and alignment.

the cutter. (This is opposite direction to that used in portable routing.) With the copy router template system, cutting and profile shaping, externally and internally, can be performed with the one template. The making of the 'snack tray' illustrated at Fig. 58, is a good example. the securing of the template to the workpiece, can be carried out in a number of ways, and we will now describe various methods.

Work-form carrier

Sometimes the template is secured by double sided tape or vacuum direct onto the workpiece, usually for profile applications.

However, a work-form carrier is more practical, and recommended by health and safety authorities. The carrier enables the workpiece to be manipulated with fingers well away from rotating cutter. Furthermore, a well designed carrier will allow for good gripping and comfortable handling for the operators benefit.

Securing the workpiece

The workpiece can be fixed down to the carrier frame by double sided tape (this will 'roll off' easily by thumb pressure afterwards), alternatively by toggle clamps, upturned pins or held by vacuum. Long workpieces can be wedged. See Figs 32–32.5, Chapter 6).

In the U.S.A., electric spot glueing is commonly used, but removing glue residue can cause damage both to workpiece and template carrier.

Vacuum chucking

The value of holding by vacuum, is grossly underestimated, and deserves special mention. Whilst a special vacuum pump is recommended for industrial applications, i.e. when vacuum is needed over long periods, the average vacuum cleaner can be connected to a vacuum chuck. The main advantage of vacuum holding is that the working area can be kept entirely free from obstructions. Neoprene self stick strip or sheeting is available approx. 2mm thick.

Circular work

For purely cutting and routing complete circular shapes, the overhead machining technique could well be described as uniquely superior to any other method.

'Spinning' technique

It is easy to realise why the spinning technique is so attractive to those concerned with producing circular objects, such as plaques, breadboards, large table mats, picture frames and the like.

We shall describe how relatively simple it is to manipulate or spin the workpiece around, under a rotating cutter.

If the workpiece is sufficiently thick to accept a fulcrum point or pin directly into its base, so much the better, otherwise a 'false' base can be fitted for this purpose.

A sliding beam trammel which can lock in different positions, is made in accordance with sketch, shown in Fig. 60.5. The upturned point or pin in the trammel is securely located in the workpiece base, and remains there throughout the operation.

By varying three criteria, a) the radius of the trammell b) the depth of cut c) the type/shape of cutter, most attractive circular shapes can be obtained from this relatively simple 'spinner' technique. See illustrations 60.4 showing an attractive cheese platter.

Remember for outside cutting or edging, spin in clockwise direction (against the direction of rotating cutter).

Machine routing

A natural application for the stationary router is straight forward routing or machine work. An adjustable side fence, factory made or home made, is secured by clamps or bolts to the routing table surface.

For rebating, routing and edging, the overhead machining system can be invaluable. The main limitation, is the size of the worktable, since long workpieces are inclined to tip. This can be partially overcome by clamping an extension to the existing table to increase the working surface area.

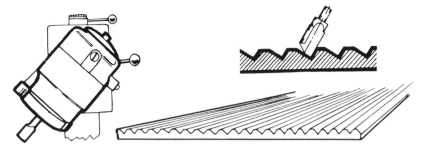

Fig.58.4. Motor is canted to 45°, to provide angular cuts and shapes.

The routing heads of these machines can be canted to angles up to 45°. In this way, angular cuts can be made to give shapes not normally possible to achieve in other ways. See Fig. 58.4.

Making louvred panels

There is a wide range of copy routing possibilities for the 'fixed head' router, and the making of louvred panels is just one more excellent application.

A 'master' slotted template is produced (see Fig. 59) on the underside of the work-form, with slots spacings and lengths matching those required on the finished article. By fitting different sizes of cutters, housings can vary to suit the louvre dimensions.

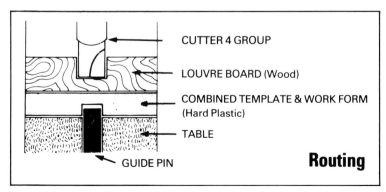

CUTTER 4 GROUP

LOUVRE BOARD (Wood)

COMBINED TEMPLATE & WORK FORM
(Hard Plastic)

TABLE

GUIDE PIN

Routing

Fig.58.5. Sketch showing the system and template method used for cutting louvre panels.

Fig.59.(a)   With   simple   device   for making louvred panels, the louvre 'master slots' are cut into the actual work-form itself.

(b) The blank louvre panels, ready for slotting, are clamped by wedges, hammered in lightly on each side.

(c) Routing out the louvre housings, using the novel workform which cuts both louvre panels from the one template.

A system for clamping the workpiece, is illustrated in Fig. 59(b), two finely tapered wedges were used, and when hammered lightly in place, provided a most effective clamping arrangement.

Production of staircase template

This overhead router, called the Trend 11/30, accommodates most heavy duty hand routers in the head frame. It simulates the basic actions of the high performance sophisticated routers, but at a fraction of the cost.

The project seen in Fig. 60, is the production of templates from dense ⅜″ laminated plastic. The templates are used by the building trades in the UK to make the treads and risers of staircases.

All slots and drilled holes, in addition to the L shaped cut-out, were made with router. Special TC counterbores were used to produce the c′board drilled holes, whilst a S3/22 TC, two flute cutter, performed all the remaining cutting work. A steel template was screwed to the base of the work-form, which had location points to ensure workpiece lined up vertically with template. Because of the stress on the guide pin, a ⁵⁄₁₆in Ø one was chosen, allowance being made for size, i.e. (⁵⁄₁₆in−¼in)÷2=¹⁄₃₂in larger all round.

Cutting was carried out with three passes through the work to avoid stress on both cutter and router.

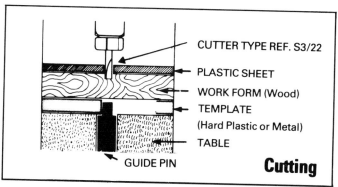

Fig.59.1. Sketch shows a cross sectional view of the copy routing system employed to cut out shapes from dense laminated plastic.

Making letters from plastic

The overhead router is commonly used by the signmaking trades, and the example of copy routing and profiling letters is fairly typical.

With acrylic, there is an inclination for material to melt and then weld itself together. Water mist spray or a fine jet of air applied to cutting point will overcome this problem.

When bevelling, use is made of the fine adjuster on the router head, to micro adjust the amount of material to be removed on the bevel.

Fig.60. A popular overhead router model 11/30 with foot pedal control for activating the router head. Application was copy routing templates used for cutting out housings for staircase treads and risers.

Fig.60.1. Cutting out and bevelling letters. With template letter E fixed to base of the 'workform' or template carrier, the perspex letter is cut from above, using a standard two flute cutter, or a one flute cutter if speed of initial cut is preferred.

Fig.60.2. With letter E cut squarely, a bevel 45deg. or 60deg. can be made, by substituting the straight cutter with a bevel cutter (refer 11 group Bevel Cutters). The workpiece itself is now used as the guide for trimming bevelled edges on the letter.

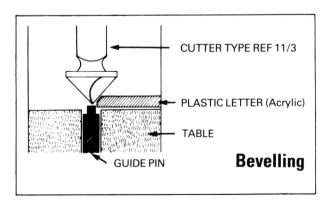

CUTTER TYPE REF 11/3

PLASTIC LETTER (Acrylic)

TABLE

GUIDE PIN

Bevelling

Fig.60.3. Sketch shows method of applying a bevelled edge to a perspex letter.

Fig.60.4. This router has a 'spinning' device mounted under the cutting head. The adjustable trammel rod allows for quick change of radii.

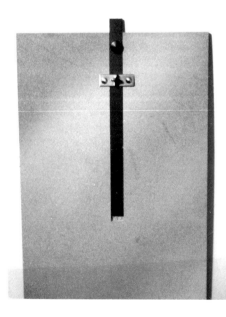

Fig.60.5. The illustration shows the separate 'spinning' board, which incorporates an adjustable trammel rod, which locks in position by a turn knob.

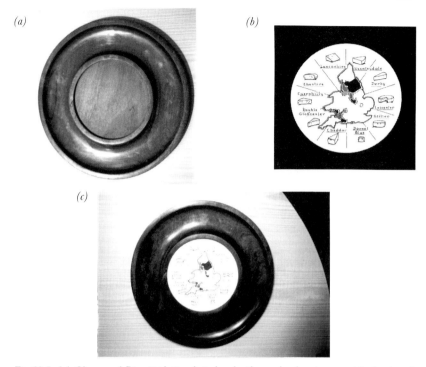

Fig.60.5. (a) Cheese and Biscuit platter shaped under the overhead router on a spinning board. The radius 'trough' was cut with a 15/1 cutter, whilst the centre part was grooved out with a 4/5 19mm (¾") cutter. (b) The 'cheese' tile slots into the central recess shown in (c). (c) Completed cheese platter. A most useful and indeed attractive project, if trouble is taken to select well grained and decorative timber.

One useful tip for template following is to mark out the approximate path which the router will be taking, with a pencil on the top of the workpiece.

Spinning circular shapes

The overhead router lends itself for producing circular objects, by virtue of the fact that ones hands can be kept free to manipulate the workpiece. Using a spinning technique with an adjustable trammel recessed into the support board, it provides the possibility of cutting and shaping such objects as platters, wall plaques, decorative panels, and discs at considerable speed. For industry, the cutting of circular gaskets, templates, and spacers on a batch production basis, is greatly simplified using this system of operation.

The workpiece rotates on a fulcrum pin, which is fitted to a sliding trammel rod recessed into the support board. The rod can be moved forwards and backwards in a matter of seconds, and locked to provide a positive radius (see Fig. 60.5).

By interchanging cutters and varying the depth, numerous possibilities are opened up for cutting, slotting and shaping operations.

Producing a shaped 'snack tray'

This could be described as a masterful example of the template system, because in this project, the one template performs four tasks, first the perimeter cutting, then with a staff bead or ovolo cutter, the moulding. Finally, the centre part of the template enables a two-flute straight cutter to remove the central part of the tray. The internal edging is then shaped with a radiused cutter.

The four cutters used, with only one change of guide pin size, are illustrated at Fig. 61.

A number of these trays were produced with the workpieces held

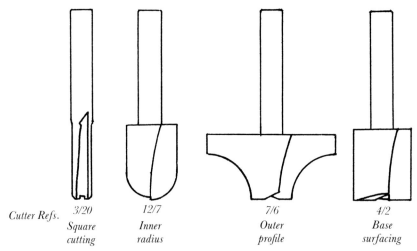

Cutter Refs.	3/20	12/7	7/6	4/2
	Square cutting	Inner radius	Outer profile	Base surfacing

Fig.61. Above cutters were interchanged for producing the 'snack tray' shown in Fig. 62.1. The one template covered all operations.

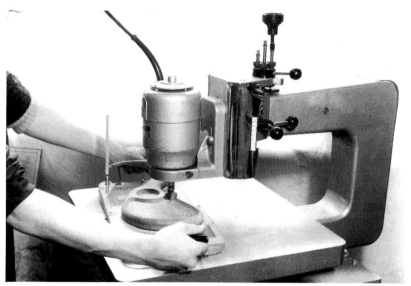

Fig.62. The overhead router is set up for batch production of the small tray. Template on base follows a guide pin. Workpiece is held down by vacuum. Refer vacuum chuck construction, Fig. 63.

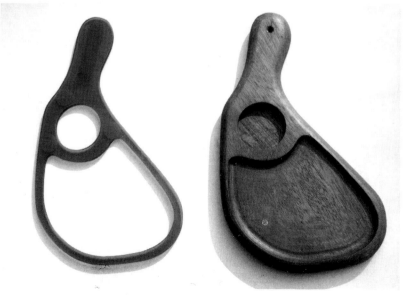

Fig.62.1. The template with finished 'snack tray' alongside.

down by toggle clamps, but vacuum clamping was found to be ideal, giving clear view for operating. Toggle clamps were found to upset the continuity of routing, as they needed to be repositioned from time to time.

Vacuum clamping

Vacuum clamping can be applied in a number of ways, but the method of producing the vacuum chuck for this particular operation is illustrated at Fig. 63, and shows the components in exploded view. (Refer to appendix for source of supply.)

There are certain shortcomings with the conventional system for clamping of the workpiece. Often toggle clamps hinder the operator's movement and vision. It becomes necessary to move the clamps to a new position when profiling. Furthermore, it is most inconvenient at times to screw or pin the workpiece on to the template frame.

The vacuum system of clamping is totally underated, possibly because it is not a mechanical device, and therefore suspect. The holding power of a small vacuum pump is quite astonishing. The small pump shown in Fig. 64.2 is approx. 1ft. long and has a vacuum displacement of 17psi. A vacuum chuck area of say, 1ft×1ft will hold a workpiece down with a suction factor, which would prevent the workpiece from being prised off without considerable effort.

Vacuum chuck construction

There are certain rules to which one must adhere when making a vacuum chuck, and visual sketches describe them more effectively.

The larger the exposed area to vacuum the more efficient will be the holding power.

The three diagrams A, B and C, illustrate this point clearly:

Thin workpiece unsupported.

X

(A) *Wrong*
Thin material has bowed with the vacuum.
Small pads are needed to support central area.

*Poor vacuum feed to work-
piece, no effective seal.*

(B) *Wrong*
Support pads are too large
reducing vacuum area to
unacceptable limits.

X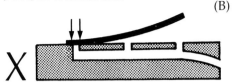

*Good vacuum with large chuck
area and centre supports if
material thin & likely to buckle.*

(C) *Right*
Large vacuum area with small
pads.

√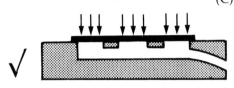

Sealant material for vacuum

This is offered in narrow strip form (in rolls, see Fig. 63.1), or in sheet
form for cutting with a sharp knife.

The self-adhesive backed neoprene should be 1.5–2.5mm thick. It
must be the closed cell variety. If thicker material was used, vibration
could arise and a poor finished edge result.

The neoprene strip (see Fig. 63.1) is normally 16mm wide and can
be cut easily into lengths, with reliable joints made by overlapping
and then cutting both layers with 'razor' knife. The vented hole
(3mm–8mm dia) can be anywhere within the chuck area. Small cut
strips may be needed to provide support pads, to prevent workpiece
from bowing.

Neoprene sheet, can be applied in a quite ingenious manner by
using the router to profile cut the shape. Assuming the template has
been affixed to the chuck base, the procedure is as follows. Remove
adhesive backing, and apply a sheet of neoprene across the proposed
chuck area. now make a profile cut, with cutter depth set to penetrate
neoprene plus approx. 1mm. Following the template path, the
neoprene pattern is obtained in a matter of seconds. The waste
material can be peeled off quite easily, if this is done within a few
hours of applying the material.

Listed procedures for building a vacuum chuck.

(1) Workpiece.
(2) Work frames are glued or fixed together with double-sided tape.
(3) Two ¼″ dia. holes drilled in top frame to line up with—
(4) Channel routed out in bottom work frame to link up with—
(5) Hose connector (Threaded ⅛b.s.p. ¼b.s.p. into top half of work frame.
(6) Plastic vacuum tube leading to pump
(7) Neoprene lip seal with self-adhesive backing is cut to length. See Fig. 63.1.
(8) Template glued with double sided adhesive to underside of work frame.
(9) Guide pin must line up with cutter, and should not project more than thickness of template.

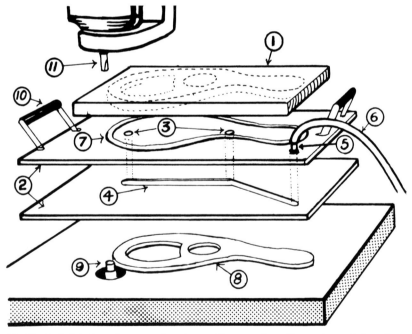

Fig.63. Exploded view of vacuum clamping set illustrates how this can be carried out in an efficient manner.

Fig.63.1. Neoprene strip with self stick backing 16mm wide. 2mm app. thick.

Profiling using vacuum for holding

For purely profile cutting and edging small components, the use of vacuum to hold down the workpiece is a more efficient means of working.

The template itself is converted into a vacuum chuck, by applying self-stick neoprene sheeting to it.

The chuck/template, which is a replica of the end product, should be made of a relatively hard matter, e.g. Acrylic, PVC, or Tufnol. Vacuum is obtained from a vacuum pump or a commercial vacuum extractor.

Fig. 64 describes one system for profiling with vacuum.

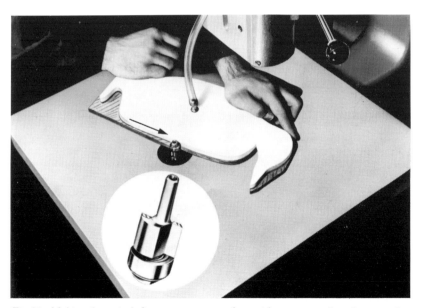

Fig.64. Making 'penguins' from a perspex template with vacuum pad on lower surface. Vacuum is vented by central 1/4 BSP itting with vacuum pump mounted overhead. Note the guide bearing trimming cutter ref. 46/2. Direction of feed is shown by arrow.

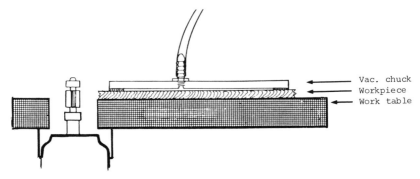

                                                                    Vac. chuck
                                                                    Workpiece
                                                                    Work table

Fig.64.1. Diagram showing the vacuum system for profiling with router inverted. Guide bearing trimmer (right) Ref. 46/2 is commonly used for such operations.

Fig.64.2. A small Typical Vacuum Pump which has 17psi Extraction rate, is supplied complete with foot pedal on/off switch. Size approx. 12in long, 8in high.

14   Mobile routing heads

Panel tracking router

A new innovation for the building industry, and for all those needing to machine or cut large sheets of material, is a panel tracking machine. So called, because the machine head, incorporating a saw or router, is conveyed along a track up to 8ft long.

The advantage of propelling a machine head mounted on a roller bearing track to machine the work, can only be really described by the operator, who has also used the conventional method. The handling of a large sheet, be it plywood or chipboard, is fatigueing, irrespective of the effort required to pass it through a fixed saw or router head.

Clamps for holding the workpiece, and limit stops can be supplied to order.

Copy pantograph carving machine

This machine is based on the conventional pantograph concept, but less sophisticated, and designed to accept small routers up to 650 watts.

Called the 'Brisklathe' Carving Machine, it is designed for the serious amateur and those involved in small batch repetition work. The basic model reproduces on a 1:1 rating basis, but an attachment enables reductions to be cut, should this be required.

The setting up and putting to work, is straightforward. Templates are mounted in a frame, and the workpiece is centred and clamped in an adjustable work holder. To operate, the stylus is lowered into the template groove and the cutter into the material. With the stylus

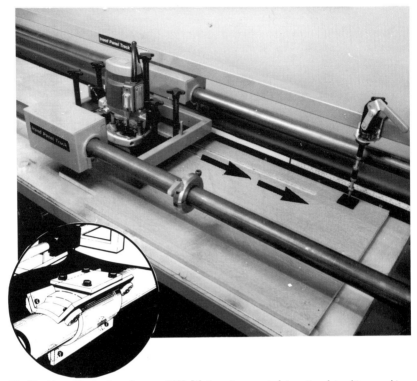

Fig.65. Above illustration shows a 1600 Watt router mounted in a panel tracking machine. Height adjustment is obtained by the fine depth rod on the router. Note the clamp for holding the workpiece and limit stop on the runner bars. Inset shows the two sets of three roller bearings, which provide a precision and free running capability.

following the template, an exact repetition of the pattern is reflected in the workpiece. Small router cutters with ¼in Ø shanks can be used with this machine.

Router mounted on radial arm saw

The 'Dewalt' radial arm saws have the facility to accept the Black and Decker routers. Adaptors could be produced for other makes of routers, if the problem is passed to a competent engineer.

The advantages of an overhead router for certain applications have already been described in the previous chapters. However, the

Fig.65.1. Pantograph 'Brisk-lathe' Carving Machine with Elu Mof 96 mounted.

conversion of a radial arm saw into an overhead router could be an attractive proposition, for those who already possess one. Remember though, only light machining jobs can be performed with a router under 1000 watts rating.

Fig.65.2. Dewalt radial arm saw is seen fitted with a B and D router which has been mounted alongside the saw motor.

15 Care, maintenance and safety precautions

Previous writings on the 'plunging' router have neglected to emphasise the importance of the cutter, or router bit as it is called. One experienced craftsman in this field says: 'The hand router is only as good as the cutter used in it.' How true this is! A feathery edge on the board is more likely to have been caused by a blunt cutter than a faulty machine.

Selecting cutters

A wide range of cutters in numerous shapes and sizes is on the market and a special wallchart which describes these in an informative manner can be supplied (parts of this chart are reproduced in the Appendix). A brief run down of the various types of cutters follows below.

Straight cutters: these are cutters with single or double flutes, straight edged, and leaving a 90 deg. cut edge.

Shaped cutters: these are used mainly for moulding, bevelling, shaping and panelling.

Grades of cutters: by grades of cutters, we are referring to the metallurgical composition. We will describe for simplicity, the two main types available for hand routing machines.

High speed steel cutters

When they are sharp they will give an exceedingly good finish to the work, but if the material is abrasive in any way, they quickly become blunt and need re-sharpening after a short run of work. The materials which come under the category of non-abrasive as follows: most natural soft woods, pvc, and acrylic (non-tinted variety). It should be noted that these cutters normally have a back clearance angle of not less than 15 deg. If sharpening is to be carried out, this angle should be maintained to ensure good cutting performance.

Tungsten carbide cutters

These are greatly superior to high speed steel cutters, by virtue of their lasting quality. They are particularly suitable for harder abrasive materials, such as plywood, chipboard, hardboard, glass fibre reinforced plastics, and acrylics (tinted variety). While the complete cutter can be made out of solid tungsten carbide, the normal practice is to braze small sections of tungsten carbide onto all cutting edges (see Fig. 66).

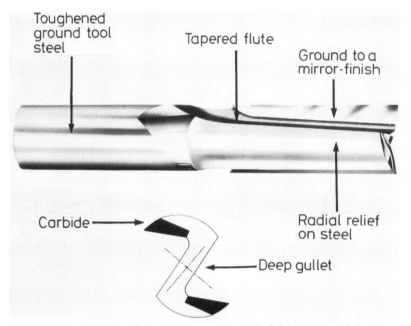

Fig.66. A typical TCT two-flute cutter in tungsten carbide. Solid tungsten carbide cutters are also available. While more expensive than the tipped variety, they can be resharpened many times before being discarded. They also have a better 'plunge' facility.

The cost of tungsten carbide cutters are, from experience, two to three times that of an HSS cutter, but they last many times as long, depending on the material. Since the time spent in removing the cutter, having it re-sharpened, and refitting it into position, has to be taken into consideration, it is generally more economical from a time saving point of view to use tungsten carbide tipped cutters. They keep their cutting edge much more efficiently and preclude the need for constant resharpening. When tungsten carbide cutters are worn, they should be re-sharpened properly at the correct angle. This too will increase their life span. Cutter maintenance is discussed fully below.

Design factor in a tungsten carbide cutter: the brazing in of the tungsten carbide insert, and the fine grinding of the insert, are important factors in a TC cutter, but the relief and clearance has to be correct if efficient cutting is to be obtained before regrinding becomes necessary.

Solid tungsten cutters

While all the advantages of tungsten tipped cutters apply equally to cutters made completely from tungsten, the solid TC cutters have an additional advantage in that they are less likely to snap under stress because they are ground from a single piece of steel. Their plunge facility is also superior. Cost is, however, somewhat higher than the tipped TC cutters.

Diamond bonded cutters

A new development whereby diamond crystals, bonded to carbide under high pressure and intense heat, has resulted in cutters outlasting normal carbide ones, many times over.

However, at the present time, they are extremely expensive, and only attractive to the large furniture manufacturers, when the delay in changing tools for resharpening, needs to be obviated.

Maintenance

Generally speaking it is advisable to send cutters to a reputable cutter sharpening firm, as accurate equipment is needed to refurbish the cutters to a standard as near as possible to their original condition. However, with high speed steel cutters, hand honing with a fine stone can be carried out on the inside flat edge of the cutter, never on the outside radius, as this will alter the clearance angle and ruin the performance. It should be remembered that honing is purely a touching-up operation, and if done regularly after each short to medium run of work, the cutter will give excellent results over a long period. If the cutter is allowed to deteriorate honing will be ineffective, and it will need to be sent to a specialist for regrinding.

The merit in having one's cutters resharpened by a firm with specialised equipment cannot be over-emphasised. So often it is thought that there is a short cut to this problem, and the end results of this attitude are shown clearly in Fig. 66.3. Fig. 66.4 shows how the same cutter appears after it has been reground correctly. Note the excellent relief for clearance of chips.

Re-grinding attachments are available for some hand routers. With these it is possible to sharpen straight cutters effectively, but the setting up of the apparatus is most important, and only a minimal amount of material should be ground off at any one time. Cutting angles must be maintained if success is to be achieved.

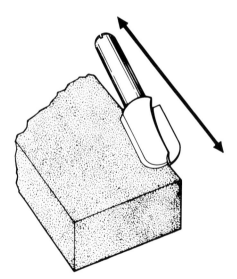

Fig.66.1. High speed steel cutters can be honed by hand on a fine slip stone. Only the inside flat edges should be honed, never on the outside.

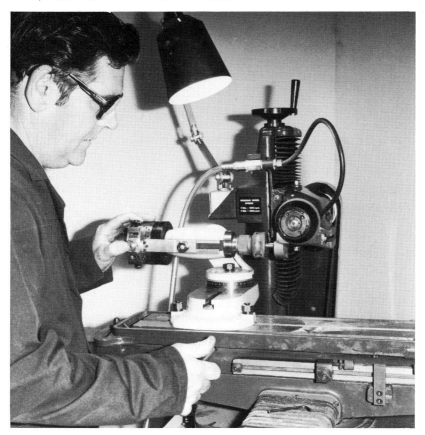

Fig.66.2. Cutters being serviced on premises of a saw doctor. They should be reground correctly when their edges have become dull. A cutter needs attention when the cut edge becomes 'feathery' or when the motor is dropping its revs unusually.

Re-sharpening of TCT cutters should not be attempted at all without the correct equipment. Special diamond-impregnated grinding wheels are used by firms with equipment which ensures the correct reliefs are maintained. Each firm charges a different rate for the job, but providing the tungsten tip is still intact, the cost for sharpening is approximately £2.00 a time.

It is not generally realised that the shanks of router cutters should be maintained smooth, and as near to the condition as received from the factory. A cutter shank with a burr on it will result in an inaccurate cut

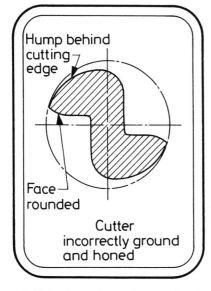

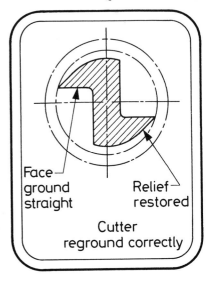

Fig.66.3. Cutter incorrectly ground and honed.

Fig.66.4. Cutter reground correctly.

and may also cause vibration. With the larger cutters bearings on the motor may be adversely affected owing to the inbalance. Over-tightening of the collet often distorts it, and causes grooves in the cutter shank. Dirt or grit adhering to the shank will have a similar effect. It is therefore important that the cutter shank is regularly examined.

Feed speed relative to work

It is important to look after your routing machine by not overloading it. A clear sign that the machine is being overloaded is a drastic drop in the revolutions of the spindle. Feed rate therefore can be judged by the sound of the motor. In time the operator will acquire a 'feel' for the router, and a feed speed relative to the work will come to him naturally. It will be found that a narrow cutter can be used at a higher speed than a wider one.

A guide line for assessing cutting depth is that the depth of cut should not exceed the diameter of the cutter. If this principle is not adhered to when routing hard material the cutter may snap. If the cutter is inclined to burn the material it is a sign that either the cutter is blunt or that the feed speed is too slow.

It is impossible to give a hard and fast rule about recommended cutting speeds because conditions vary from job to job. Generally speaking, however, a ¼in. diameter cutter requires a free running speed of between 20,000 and 24,000 rpm for the best results. Conversely, a cutter of ¾in. diameter needs a speed of between 14,000 and 20,000 rpm. An important point to remember is that if the router is underpowered the cutting speed under load will be drastically reduced and a poor performance is the obvious result. A correct periphery speed using a sharp cutter will ensure a good finish. A feathery finish on the groove edges is the usual sign that attention is needed in this area. Several passes with the router should be made if a single deep pass causes the revs. to drop below 70 per cent of the free running speed.

Routers should always be fed in the opposite direction to that in which the cutter is rotating. Fig. 66.5 shows the direction of feed when the router is overhead, i.e. in portable routing/profiling. When using a fixed head router (spindle) with the cutter pointing upwards through the table, the material is fed in the opposite direction.

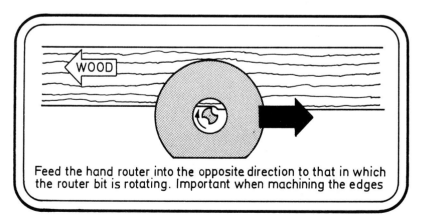

Feed the hand router into the opposite direction to that in which the router bit is rotating. Important when machining the edges

Fig.66.5. Important: whether for portable working or when using the router on the machine stand, the direction of feed must oppose the cutter direction when profiling.

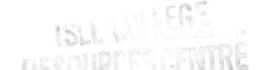

TECHNIQUES OF ROUTING

To summarise then, there are five important points to consider when using a router to achieve the best results:

Don't feed the router too slowly as it will burn the material rather than cut it;

Don't overtighten the collet chuck;

Don't feed the router too fast. The finish will be inferior.

Don't overload the motor, but keep up the motor revolutions.

Don't try to service the router yourself; send it to an accredited service agent.

Safety precautions

It would be wrong to exclude the question of safety precautions, which should be taken when routing. These are listed as under, and should be included under do's and don'ts.

Do fit a light mask over your nose and mouth, when routing for a lengthy period.

Do wear ear muffs, when routing with the larger models in a confined space.

Do use protective goggles when routing particle boards and aluminium.

Do switch off and preferably unplug the router when changing cutters or accessories: an elementary precaution, but so often ignored.

16 Projects

PROJECT A – Reproducing period furniture

The project is a 17th century carved chair – Chippendale style, with upholstered drop-in seat. Illustrations show mastercraftsman Neil Batchelor at work, when extensive use was made of a 3/4 horse power hand router.

We are not suggesting that the router can replace the expertise needed to make period style furniture, but we will show how the router can relieve the craftsman from much of the 'slogging work'.

The difference between the routing techniques used for this Chippendale reproduction, and that employed for conventional applications, is fairly basic. Normally the router is a finishing tool with edges needing little or no further attention, apart from light sanding.

With hand made furniture, when chairs are made singly in period styles, with no one piece being identical to another, the router is applied in a different manner. You will note that extensive use has been made of the router, but the router is applied more to remove waste wood, rather than produce a finished edge. In other words, finishing still requires skilled hand work.

Selection of timber and marking out

With the difficulty in obtaining really seasoned timber, Mr Batchelor chose to use discarded mahogany sections taken from old furniture, roof structures etc.

Planning was not based on working from accurate drawings. He followed the system used by master craftsmen of by-gone days, in so

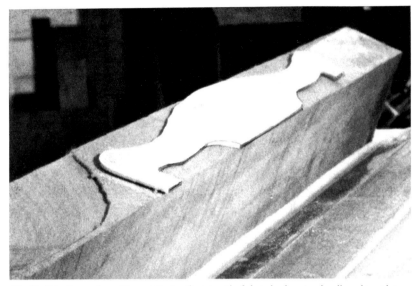

Fig.67. Selecting and marking out timber for top rail of chair back, using hardboard template.

far as rough sketches were made of intended design. Chalk marks were made on the timber for selecting the 'best cuts', (i.e., selecting the right colour and grade), prior to rough sawing the components on a bandsaw. Some components were marked out using hardboard templates.

Cutting and machining

Using a bandsaw, shapes were cut with sufficient waste but not excessive. The areas of work, where the router became invaluable, are illustrated in Fig. 68, the seat rails and front legs were shaped with the router, but the arms themselves were spoke-shaved by hand. The rebates in the seat area were all cut for the router. He further used the router in conjunction with the template (see Fig. 67.1) to rough cut the left scalloped shapes of the back splats on the chair. The right hand matching pattern was obtained by reversing the template.

Mr Batchelor developed certain routing skills of an unusual nature, for he applied the router in the form of a surfacing tool, using it free hand – see illustration 68.1. Careful sweeping movements were

Fig.67.1. Marking out the first cuts for bandsawing. Note the templates in the foreground.

made, when up to 3mm of material was removed at one time. Considerable skill and practice is needed for this free hand work, and a sharp cutter is essential. The final shaping and finishing of the back

Fig.67.2. Applying an ovollo mould to the seat rails using the router and side fence.

splats was carried out with chisel, scraper, file and sand-paper.

With the limited space available, it is impossible to do justice and describe fully the immense skill involved, in the preparatory work, the

Fig.68. First assembly of seat rail and arm support. Note the moulded seat rail and the support member which has been carved and shaped by hand.

design, the shaping and final assembling. Even the glueing and clamping require special skills, for instance, the chair back, front rail and legs are usually assembled and glued first in order to simplify the

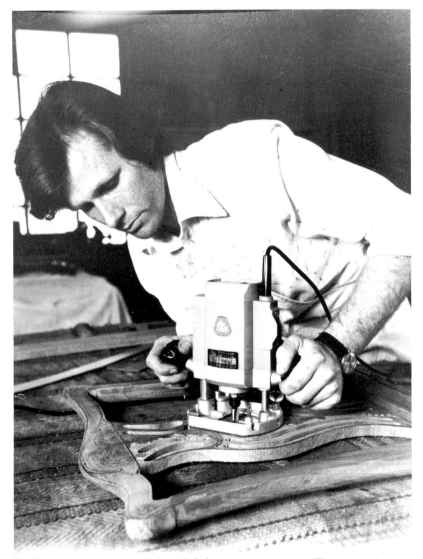

Fig.68.1. Surfacing the chair back, with light sweeping movements. This unusual free hand working requires considerable practice.

final assembly and clamping operation. Fig. 68.2 shows the first 'mock assembly' of the chair's components. Note that there is still hand shaping required on left hand arm rest.

Fig.68.2. Chair components assembled, prior to glueing and clamping. Note the left arm rest which still requires hand shaping.

PROJECT B – Building a staircase

There are three basing methods for stair trenching.

The hand way

Cutting the strings by hand with mallet, chisel, and tenon saw, is the method taught at school, but it will be impossible to make a living this way.

The mechanical way

For really fast trenching, a stair housing machine is available, but a spindle moulder is the most commonly used machine for staircase work. However, the spindle moulder is often occupied, and 'breaking it down' and resetting it again for under three flights of stairs, is not usually economical.

The middle-of-the-road way

There is now a well proven and efficient way of cutting stairstrings with a hand router. For an outlay of £75 (£100 with cutters) a stair template device for use with any heavy duty router, can be obtained. Whilst detailed instructions are provided on purchase of the template, information about the actual making of a staircase, using this device, has not been published so far.

Stan Coombs of Bickerton and Son Ltd., of St. Albans, has made a number of staircases with the Trend template (Fig. 69) and his knowledge on the subject is extensive.

To commence with though, for the benefit of those not familiar with building regulations, some basic restrictions about stair design should be brought to your notice.

Building Regulations UK only re: staircases

The fullest information about these matters can be obtained from your

Fig.69. The Trend Stair Jig Mk. IV.

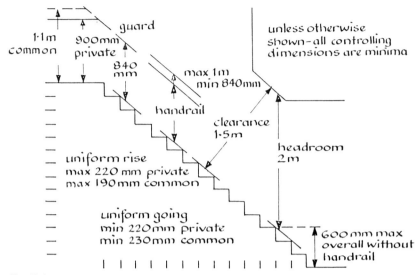

Fig.69.1. Basic staircase restrictions described above.

Local Authority. Sometimes, one can obtain a waiver on regulations, if old staircases are being replaced, but the diagram on Fig. 69.1 provides the basic information, which should be carefully observed.

Stan Coombs will now describe in his own words, the procedure for building a staircase.

Measuring up for the staircase

Consider carefully the direction of approach to the proposed staircase, especially where it will finish, bearing in mind any door or window openings.

If a drawing has not been provided, I always first draw a simple line plan with an elevation scale 1-20. This allows you to measure off all required timber, (i.e. length of strings, handrails and newells). The sketch will show if I have allowed enough headroom, also whether the components will assemble together without snags.

To assess the amount of rise accurately, use a storey rod. The total rise being the height of finish floor to finish floor. This should be marked on a batten and then divided into required number of risers using a pair of dividers. The going is not usually the most important point to watch, but the rise must be correct.

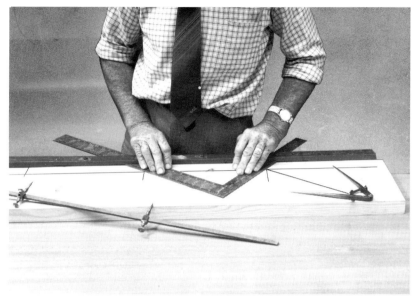

Fig.69.2. Marking out the strings, using roofing square, dividers, and Beam Trammels.

Setting up a roofing square, refer Fig. 69.2

With a wooden fence attached, set the rise and going on it, using a gauge line as a margin.

This can also be used for marking tenons, newels and floor lines.

Setting out a string without newels

First check which side will give the best appearance: remember, the wall string will be seen on one side only. If there is a bow in its length, then put this uppermost and to quote an old saying "Bible side up". Now gauge the bottom edge of the string for the margin. I use a 42mm margin, which, when using a normal 'rise and going', leaves a reasonable space between nosing and edge of string. Next, mark off the floor line, and using a beam compass or a pair of large dividers (setting it to the pitch size) step off the required number of treads and risers. The last one will be the top nosing.

Square these lines over and on to the other string. If a newel is

Fig.69.3. Checking correct spacings – before clamping up.

required, it is easy to set this out using the square, bearing in mind the face of the riser will be the centre of the newel.

Setting up the template and router (Fig. 69.3)

The Trend template is placed on the timber, fence side downwards and set on the marked out string. The correct spacing between the cutter and edge of the template must not be overlooked.

For this purpose, a strip of plywood is used to represent the difference between the part to be cut away and the template slot width.

Once set in position, the template fence is adjusted and made fast against the top edge of the string (see Fig. 69.4). Adjust the sliding follower 'nose' piece on the base plate, to suit the required overhang for the tread nosing (see Fig. 69.5). The dovetail cutters are in tungsten carbide (tipped) and have an angle of 95°. The cutter I chose for this work is a Trend (ref 32/1) which is the one recommended for a 1" (nomimal) tread thickness. The router depth device is set to cut to a

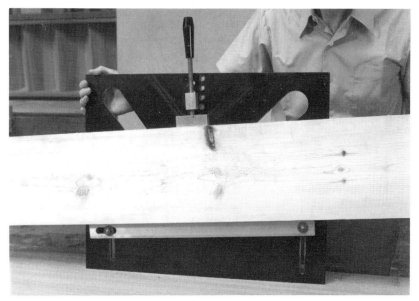

Fig.69.4. Sighting of clamping system from below workpiece.

depth of 12mm below the template, and this can be done in one pass. Now that the template and router have been set up, the next procedure is to position the template on the string for cutting. The template is aligned on the marked out string by using ply spacers, and then it is clamped.

Machining the strings

Switch on router and plunge to present 12mm depth. Commence routing the first riser, keeping to left hand side and returning down the riser on right hand side. See Figs 69.6, 69.7 and 69.8. Repeat this procedure for the tread. It is advisable to cut in this sequence; remember the feed of the router should oppose the rotation of the cutter when profiling.

Fig.69.5. Special base plate, with adjustable nosing and cutter fitted (Ref. 32/1).

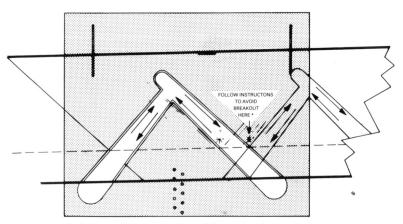

FOLLOW INSTRUCTONS
TO AVOID
BREAKOUT
HERE *

Fig.69.6. Sketch showing sequence to be observed for routing risers and treads

Fig.69.7. Routing out the riser first, before the tread.

Fig.69.8. Routing out the tread, having completed the riser.

Routing the second string

It is essential to move the template up from left to right on both strings when repositioning. This will ensure there is no break-out at*, see Fig. 69.6. Line up the template as for first string, and repeat clamping and routing procedures.

Special note in respect of cutters recommended

Tread thickness	Recommended cutter
⅞in thick	32/10
1in thick	32/1
1⅛in thick	32/2
1¼in thick	32/3

Machining opposing strings

The fence can be fitted on the other side of the jig without the inconvenience of resetting when machining the opposing string.

Fig.69.9. Treads and risers trimmed, assembled and secured with glued angle blocks.

Fig.69.10. Checking angle of strings against Newel.

Fig.69.11. Fitting the treads and risers into the strings.

Fig.69.12. Flight of stairs has been assembled and clamped with folding wedges.

Remove back fence bar by removing hexagon nuts only. Replace on opposite side of jig and tighten up. Remove clamp fixing bolt and replace clamp on other side of jig.

Fig.69.13. When treads are tight, wedges are glued and driven in hard.

Assembly of treads and risers

Treads and risers are cut to length and fitted together using glued angle blocks (Fig. 69.9). These can now be fitted into the strings separately and remember the width of each tread must be accurately marked at each end and superfluous wood planed off.

A useful means for testing the angles of strings and hand rails relative to newels, is to set a section of plywood up to it, marking it off the roofing square (69.10).

The stairs can now be assembled, strutting off the roof or from bench cramps. See Fig. 69.12. Ensure the assembly is square and 'out of twist'.

Check all treads are really tight, and only then wedge up and screw through the rises into the tread. Wedge the riser first, then follow with the tread wedging.

Note that wedges should be well glued and driven in hard. See Fig. 69.13.

Summing up

You will realise that only an outline of staircase construction can be described in this available space, but using Mr. Coombs practical experience in making staircases, we hope the information provided will assist you.

A template for 'open' staircases is shortly to be in production, please contact the Trend organisation.

PROJECT C – Dovetailing with template jig

This jig offered for the Elu router, can be used with most other routers, by fitting an adaptor plate to the base.

The maximum working width is 300mm (approx. 12″). Board thickness acceptable – minimum 12mm, maximum 30mm.

This jig should be mounted on a bench, with allowance made for the vertical mounted dovetailed board, so jig base plate should be just proud of the work table front.

Fit guide bush to router, and the dovetail cutter supplied. A gauge is provided to ensure the cutter extends correctly – see Fig. 70.1. However, a fine depth adjuster accessory is used to obtain the cutter projection exactly as required (see Fig. 70).

Clamping-in the wood sections

Refer to Fig. 70.9 for plan of dovetailing and assembly. The front and the back of the drawer will be boards marked B, and side boards are marked A.

The boards are clamped against stops using frontal knobs to secure vertical board A and top knobs to secure horizontal board.

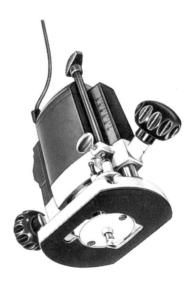

Fig.70. Router fitted with dovetail cutter and guide bush, which will engage in the dovetail fingers. The fine adjuster rod is needed to give the exact projection. See Fig. 70.1.

Fig.70.1. The fine adjuster rod is rotated fractionally if the setting guage shown here demands it. (15mm is normal projection from base.)

The top of the vertical board must be flush with horizontal one. The dovetail finger plate is now clamped in position.

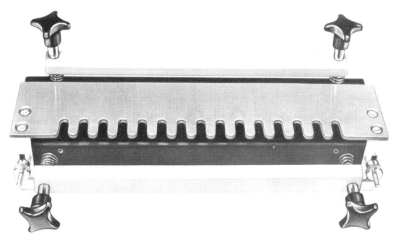

Fig.70.2. The dovetail jig which enables the dovetail tongues and grooves to be cut simultaneously.

Fig.70.3. A dovetailed corner joint produced by the router and the dovetail jig illustrated at Fig. 70.2.

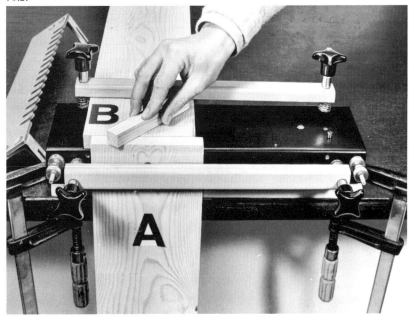

Fig.70.4. Clamp the two boards A (side board) and B (front or back) in the dovetailing attachment with their inner sides facing outwards. The two boards should touch each other and their top surfaces should be flush.

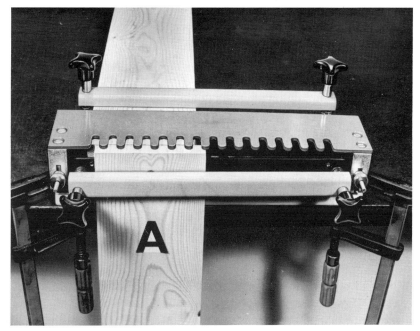

Fig.70.5. Now lay the dovetailing template on top, position it correctly and tighten the knurled nuts at either end.

Using the router

Now place the router on the dovetailing template (with the cutter and bush within the fingers). Switch on the motor and working from left to right, engage the router so that the guide bush passes between the fingers of the template. Pass it over the full width of the template keeping the guide bush in contact with the template at all times.

Since good tight fitting joints depend on accurate setting, it is advisable to make trial cuts first.

Adjustments should be made as under, if the joints are not found to be satisfactory.

Dovetail joint is too loose
Remedy: Increase depth of cutter half a millimetre at a time.

Dovetail joint is too tight
Remedy: Decrease depth of cutter half a millimetre at a time.

Fig.70.6. With the cutter and bush running within the fingers, and working from left to right, the dovetails are cut simultaneously in the ends of both boards.

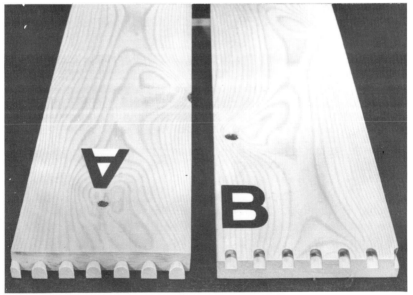

Fig.70.7. Take the two boards A and B out of the dovetailing attachment and join them together.

Dovetail is too shallow
Remedy: Unscrew fractionally the two knurled nuts on each side, and bring finger plate assembly forward. Retighten nuts.

Dovetail joint is too deep
Remedy: Reverse procedure above, i.e. move finger plate assembly back fractionally.

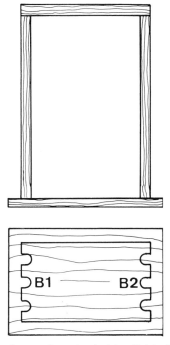

Fig.70.8. A rebated drawer front can be produced with a slightly different procedure. Details are supplied with instructions from supplier.

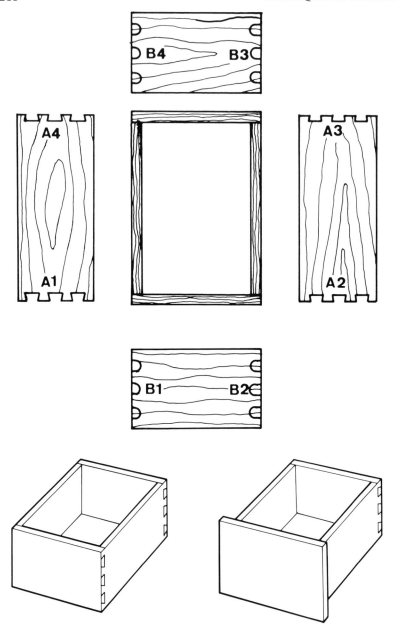

Fig.70.9. Assembly plans.

PROJECT D – Making a guitar

Handmade guitars are becoming increasingly in demand for their individuality. It follows a trend towards a rebuff of things mass produced.

A custom made electric guitar will cost some hundreds of pounds, depending on the degree of uniqueness and the purse of the buyer.

Gordon Adams, designer and craftsman has volunteered to pass on his method of producing custom built guitars with emphasis on his dependence on the router to perform his machining work. The electric guitar, unlike many stringed instruments, if often produced from solid natural wood.

A number of hardwoods are suitable, but careful selection relative to strength, seasoning, grain and colour must all be born in mind. These factors are considered in conjunction with musical performance, when the expertise and experience of Mr. Adams is of paramount importance.

Applications for the router – (summarised 1–6)

1) Profile shaping of the body after rough bandsawing blank, and planing to thickness.
2) Rebating the corner edge of body to receive decorative binding.
3) Recessing slots to accept electronic pick-ups and control panel.
4) Routing out slot in body to receive neck (neck joint).
5) Slotting a groove along the neck to receive the tension rod.
6) Shaping the pegboard to a pattern.

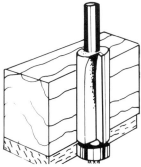

Long reach self-guide cutter for profiling body Ref. 46/22

Self-guide cutter with bearing guide mounted on shank for profiling peg board Ref. 46/90

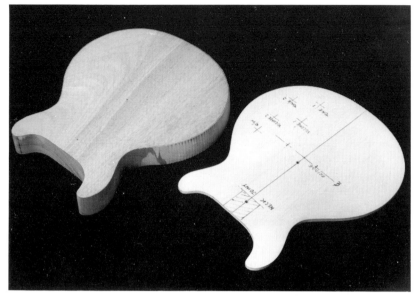

Fig.71. (Left) Body, rough bandsawed and ready for trimming. (Right) Template ready for screwing to top face.

Preparation and machining (refer Figs 71–71.10)

We shall now describe how the router was applied to perform the applications summarised in 1–6 on previous page.

Templates

The first procedure following selection of timber was to make by hand, the templates which will be needed for all the machining operations. They must be accurate and smooth, since imperfections, will naturally be reflected in the finished components. (Convex errors can be remedied, concave ones could be a disaster.)

Template material should be between 6mm and 8mm thick, and made from hard material, but not steel, as this is inclined to cause vibrations (it will not absorb the minute eccentric rotations conveyed to the cutter from the collet). Tufnol plastic or really dense hardboard such as Masonite, is excellent. The latter was chosen for this project.

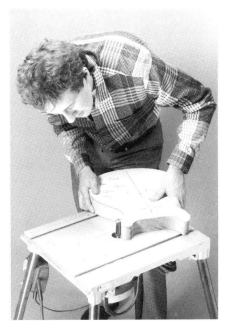

Fig.71.1. Edge of body is seen being trimmed on a routing machine table. The long reach cutter, ref. 46/22, has a guide bearing on its extremity. The follows the template mounted onto top face of body.

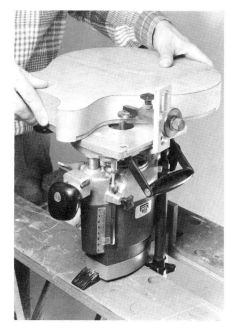

Fig.71.2. A rebate for the body binding is machined once more with router inverted. The fine micro adjuster on the router, follows the edge of the body which has already been machined. A standard square edge edge cut, ref. 3/7, was used for the light profiling work.

Machining the body

The next step is to use the appropriate template to mark out the body shape on the wood, then bandsaw the blank, not less than 2mm larger than finish size and preferably not more than 3mm. Remember, the least stock removed when machining, makes for less feed pressure and better finish. Notwithstanding the raising of unnecessary dust. The machining was carried out on a purpose made Router Table. Routers used should be heavy duty ones, 1,200 watts or above, with a collet of ⅜″ or ½″ capacity. They should have fine vertical feeds, as fine depth adjustment is of importance for all machining work on this project.

The router was fitted beneath the table, with long reach cutter projecting upwards. The cutter recommended was a guide bearing cutter, which has a 50mm long cutting edges (Tungsten Carbide Tipped), with a roller guide bearing which matches the diameter of the cutter (10mm Ø). Their reference is 46/22 (see cutter Ref. sheets, Chapter 17).

The template in this instance, was screwed to the body in positions where the pick-ups were to be inserted, so screw holes were of no consequence. With router switched on, the body with template affixed was manipulated steadily in an anticlockwise direction against the cutter, with bearing engaging on the template edge. With body profiled relatively smooth, fine finishing to remove imperfections was needed for the next operation.

Rebating body edge

The decorative corner strip or binding on the body was designed to act as a protection and also produce a decorative finish.

The router was used in the inverted position once more, but a different means of guidance was employed, well illustrated in Fig. 71.2.

A micro adjusting device, was fitted to the Elu router used in the project. The roller on the adjuster followed the shape of the body, already machined and smoothed. It was set so that a narrow rebate, approx. 8mm deep and 4mm high was cut into the edge of the body, using a standard two flute TC cutter, ½″ diameter, Ref. 3/80, with bottom cut facility. Once more the body was manipulated in anti-clockwise direction (opposite to that when router is applied to the work piece).

Shaping the pegboard

A template for the pegboard end of the neck, is screwed to the workpiece. Screw positions have been selected where cover plates will hide the holes from view.

The router table is used once more for profiling the rough sawn

Fig.71.3. The pegboard at top of neck, is seen with template affixed, ready for the trimming operation.

Fig.71.4. The pegboard is seen being shaped on the router table. This time, the guide bearing is mounted on shank of cutter, and template engages bearing at table level. Cutter reference is 46/90.

Fig.71.5. The neck is grooved out within a box jig with top mounted template. The router is fitted with a 30mm guide bush, for running in the template slot. A narrow cutter 4.8mm diam., ref. 2/40, was used to cut the slot for the rod and 11mm cutter, ref. 3/7, for end slots needed for nuts.

Fig.71.6. (Left) The neck is seen with narrow slot grooved together with larger end slots for nuts. (Right) The rod, which is tensioned to offset the contraction of the guitar strings.

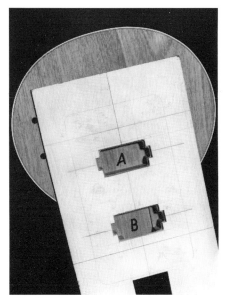

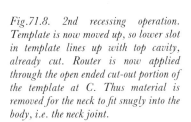

Fig.71.7. 1st recessing operation. The template is seen located over the pre-marked points, and has been stuck down with double sided tape. The hand router fitted with small 10mm guide bush and 6mm cutter now recesses the two oblong cavities to receive the pickups. See cavities A and B.

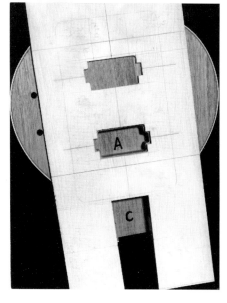

Fig.71.8. 2nd recessing operation. Template is now moved up, so lower slot in template lines up with top cavity, already cut. Router is now applied through the open ended cut-out portion of the template at C. Thus material is removed for the neck to fit snugly into the body, i.e. the neck joint.

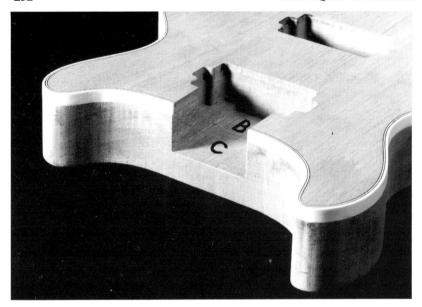

Fig.71.9. Close-up view of slot routed out in two stages, i.e. 1st operation: pick up recess at B, 2nd operation: neck joint slot recess at C.

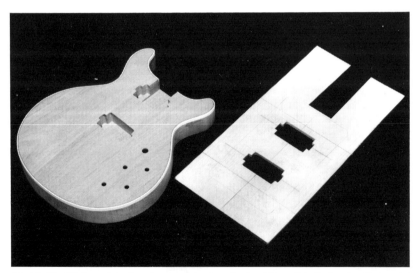

Fig.71.10. All the cavities have been routed out on the front face of the body using the template alongside. A cavity in the back of the body to receive the electric controls was recessed in a similar manner.

Fig.71.11. The neck is shown already machined for assembly and ready for hand finishing. The fret has been loosely fitted.

Fig.71.12. (Left) Guitar completed strung, tuned, and ready for playing. (Right) Basic structure machined and temporary assembled, prior to hand finishing and fitting components.

edges, but a guide bearing cutter with bearing routed on the shank end was chosen for convenience.

Cutter was Ref. 46/90. It has a 25mm cutter depth. Diameter of both cutter and bearing is 16mm. With template facing downwards on the table surface, a similar machining operation is undertaken to that of the initial body profiling work.

Making the neck

The tapered narrow part of the neck cannot be easily shaped with the router, but the slot to receive the tension rod, is a natural for the hand router. It should be explained that the neck must be under tension at all times to combat the counter tension of the guitar strings. Allowance needs therefore to be made in the slot which is to be routed. It must be gently concaved so the slot is depressed in the centre. The template is therefore concave with allowance made for the flat router base.

The conventional guide bush follower system was adopted. The slot for the guide was cut with a 5mm Ø cutter Ref. 3/1, and the slots at either end to accommodate the securing nuts, were cut with an 11mm Ø cutter Ref. 3/7. The same template and guide bush, 30mm diameter, was used in both operations. The illustration, Fig. 71.5, shows the fine vertical adjuster fitted, but for this operation, the plunge and lock system was adopted. Stops, to limit the travel, were removed for reasons of clarity, when photographing.

Cutting the cavities in the body

The frontal cavities were all cleanly cut with the router, using a template made from ¼" dense Masonite hardboard.

The template was used in two positions, as clearly described in illustrations 71.7 and 71.8. In order to negotiate the sharp corners of the cavities, a 10mm guide bush and 6mm cutter was fitted.

The back of the body, also needed a cavity to receive the electronic controls. The same routing procedure was adopted as for the frontal cavities.

17 Reference sheets

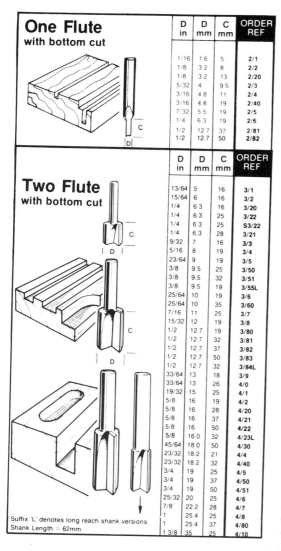

One Flute
with bottom cut

D in	D mm	C mm	ORDER REF
1/16	1.6	5	2/1
1/8	3.2	8	2/2
1/8	3.2	13	2/20
5/32	4	9.5	2/3
3/16	4.8	11	2/4
3/16	4.8	19	2/40
7/32	5.5	19	2/5
1/4	6.3	19	2/6
1/2	12.7	37	2/81
1/2	12.7	50	2/82

Two Flute
with bottom cut

D in	D mm	C mm	ORDER REF
13/64	5	16	3/1
15/64	6	16	3/2
1/4	6.3	16	3/20
1/4	6.3	25	3/22
1/4	6.3	25	S3/22
1/4	6.3	28	3/21
9/32	7	16	3/3
5/16	8	19	3/4
23/64	9	19	3/5
3/8	9.5	25	3/50
3/8	9.5	32	3/51
3/8	9.5	19	3/55L
25/64	10	19	3/6
25/64	10	35	3/60
7/16	11	25	3/7
15/32	12	19	3/8
1/2	12.7	19	3/80
1/2	12.7	32	3/81
1/2	12.7	37	3/82
1/2	12.7	50	3/83
1/2	12.7	32	3/84L
33/64	13	18	3/9
33/64	13	26	4/0
19/32	15	25	4/1
5/8	16	19	4/2
5/8	16	28	4/20
5/8	16	37	4/21
5/8	16	50	4/22
5/8	16.0	32	4/23L
45/64	18.0	50	4/30
23/32	18.2	21	4/4
23/32	18.2	32	4/40
3/4	19	25	4/5
3/4	19	37	4/50
3/4	19	50	4/51
25/32	20	25	4/6
7/8	22.2	28	4/7
1	25.4	25	4/8
1	25.4	37	4/80
1.3/8	35	25	4/10

Suffix 'L' denotes long reach shank versions.
Shank Length = 62mm.

One flute cutters – 2/1 to 2/82
These cutters are ideal for engraving and shallow work. Because of the narrow stem, extra care is needed when using the TCT version.

Two flute cutters – 3/1 to 4/80
Two flute cutters give a cleaner finish than their one flute counterparts, and at the right feed speed will give a clean cut edge to the work. Use a TCT version if material is abrasive. Solid tungsten cutters (with a prefix S) will give a better plunging cut and are less likely to snap under stress.

Ovolo cutter

The most popular of all moulding cutters because of its versatility at different depths e.g. Application for rounding over, ovollo moulding or panelling.

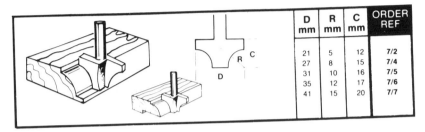

D mm	R mm	C mm	ORDER REF
21	5	12	7/2
27	8	15	7/4
31	10	16	7/5
35	12	17	7/6
41	15	20	7/7

Sash bar ovolo set

The 7/50 originally designed for sash bars, now pairs up with scribing cutter 6/50.

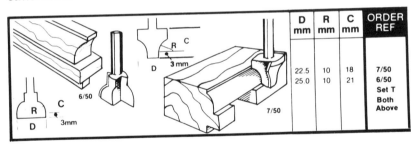

D mm	R mm	C mm	ORDER REF
22.5	10	18	7/50
25.0	10	21	6/50
			Set T
			Both
			Above

Bead classic

A multi-mould cutter with facility to give three sizes of rounding over, with bead shapes at different depths.

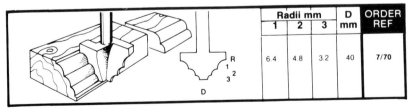

Radii mm			D mm	ORDER REF
1	2	3		
6.4	4.8	3.2	40	7/70

Classic ovolo
An attractive moulded edge for desk tops, sideboards, cupboards and clocks.

R1 mm	R2 mm	D mm	C mm	ORDER REF
7	3	26	13	7/80
10	3	30	16	7/81
13	3	35	18	7/82
15	4	38	22	7/83
19	5	44	28	7/84

Mini staff bead
This cutter offers three alternative small radii for staff beading. Ideal for edging table mats, plaques, drawer fronts, and rails on period chairs.

D mm	R mm	C mm	ORDER REF
22	4 3 2	28	9/0

Staff bead
The 9 group forms a half round bead and is decorative for rounding over edges of shelves, picture frames, table tops etc.

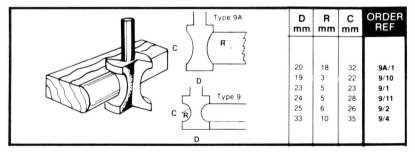

D mm	R mm	C mm	ORDER REF
20	18	32	9A/1
19	3	22	9/10
23	5	23	9/1
24	5	28	9/11
25	6	26	9/2
33	10	35	9/4

Staff bead/jointers

The 8 group provides a strong reliable tongued joint, when paired up with certain cutters in 9 group.

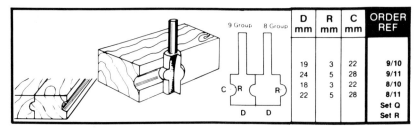

D mm	R mm	C mm	ORDER REF
19	3	22	9/10
24	5	28	9/11
18	3	22	8/10
22	5	28	8/11
			Set Q
			Set R

Staff classic bead

This cutter will produce a period style staff mould so popular with clock and cabinet makers.

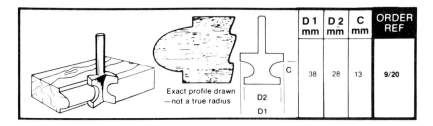

D1 mm	D2 mm	C mm	ORDER REF
38	28	13	9/20

Exact profile drawn —not a true radius

Classic staff bead

A decorative staff bead with small cove radius giving an attractive edge to table tops, sideboards etc.

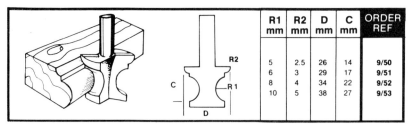

R1 mm	R2 mm	D mm	C mm	ORDER REF
5	2.5	26	14	9/50
6	3	29	17	9/51
8	4	34	22	9/52
10	5	38	27	9/53

Recess rabetter

This cutter has several applications. It produces square decorative edges but also stepped grooving for shelf supports.

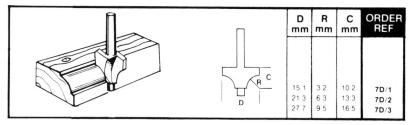

D1 mm	D2 mm	C1 mm	C2 mm	ORDER REF
12	13	8	6	36/1
14	20	8	6	36/2
16	22	8	6	36/3
13	19	8	6	36/10

Ovolo (beading) cutter with guide pin

Attractive moulds are cut on the upper edge of the board, with the guide pin following the lower part.

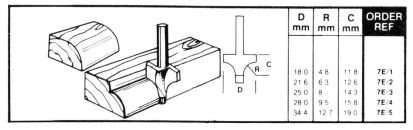

D mm	R mm	C mm	ORDER REF
15 1	3 2	10 2	7D/1
21 3	6 3	13 3	7D/2
27 7	9 5	16 5	7D/3

Rounding over cutter with guide pin

This cutter gives a plain radiused edge – with or without a top step. It is a popular moulding cutter for freehand working.

D mm	R mm	C mm	ORDER REF
18 0	4 8	11 8	7E/1
21 6	6 3	12 6	7E/2
25 0	8	14 3	7E/3
28 0	9 5	15 8	7E/4
34 4	12 7	19 0	7E/5

Rebate cutter with guide pin

A useful cutter for forming rebates as the pilot guide will easily follow small radii on shaped workpieces.

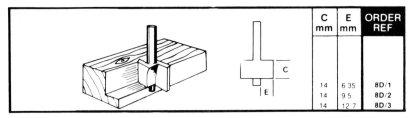

C mm	E mm	ORDER REF
14	6 35	8D/1
14	9 5	8D/2
14	12 7	8D/3

Roman ogee with guide pin

This cutter gives a decorative moulded edge, and is now increasingly popular for reproduction work.

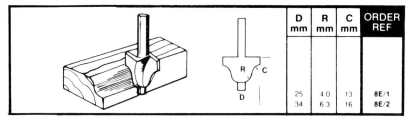

D mm	R mm	C mm	ORDER REF
25	4 0	13	8E/1
34	6 3	16	8E/2

Chamfer cutter with guide pin

Frequently used on outside sills and frames. The sign making trades use them for chamfering letters.

C mm	A	ORDER REF
13	45°	10H/1
11	30°	10H/2

Cove cutter with guide pin

Popular for edging panels, boards picture frames, and furniture.

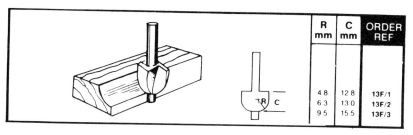

R mm	C mm	ORDER REF
4 8	12 8	13F/1
6 3	13 0	13F/2
9 5	15 5	13F/3

Chamfer 'V' groove

These cutters will chamfer boards up to 1in. thick. Having a bottom cut, they are used additionally for panelling and fluting.

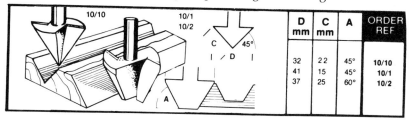

D mm	C mm	A	ORDER REF
32	22	45°	10/10
41	15	45°	10/1
37	25	60°	10/2

'V' groove and engraving

This range provides the means of freehand engraving and decorative working. Popular with those involved with fine panelling and woodcarving.

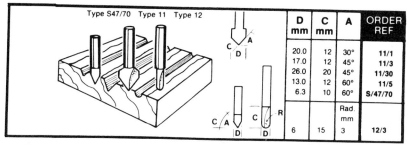

D mm	C mm	A	ORDER REF
20.0	12	30°	11/1
17.0	12	45°	11/3
26.0	20	45°	11/30
13.0	12	60°	11/5
6.3	10	60°	S/47/70
		Rad. mm	
6	15	3	12/3

Radius cutters

This range is very popular for both edging and panelling operations. Ideal for decorative finishes.

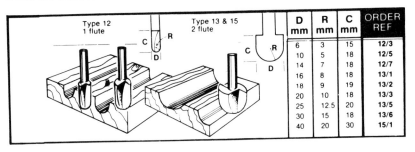

D mm	R mm	C mm	ORDER REF
6	3	15	12/3
10	5	18	12/5
14	7	18	12/7
16	8	18	13/1
18	9	19	13/2
20	10	18	13/3
25	12.5	20	13/5
30	15	18	13/6
40	20	30	15/1

Panelling

This cutter is designed for flat panelling work and gives an attractive effect on hardwood doors, cabinets etc.

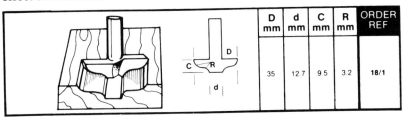

D mm	d mm	C mm	R mm	ORDER REF
35	12.7	9.5	3.2	18/1

Classic panel

These cutters offer the decorative panelling effect so sought after by those following the trend towards period style finishes.

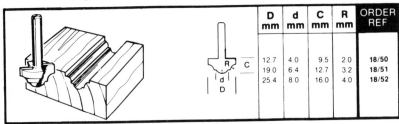

D mm	d mm	C mm	R mm	ORDER REF
12.7	4.0	9.5	2.0	18/50
19.0	6.4	12.7	3.2	18/51
25.4	8.0	16.0	4.0	18/52

Ogee mould

A popular edge mould cutter used in the furniture industry and building trades. Used shallow, across the face of the board, it offers an attractive panelling effect.

D mm	d mm	C mm	R mm	ORDER REF
27 0	8 0	16.0	4.7	**19/1**
33 50	8.0	23.0	7.20	**19/2**

Pointed round and ogee

These are ideal for fine decorative grooving, moulding and beading. Used for roping and carving on turned legs, lamp stands etc.

D mm	d mm	C mm	R mm	ORDER REF
27.0	1.0	20.0	7.50	**19/20**
13.0	1.2	12.5	4.0	**11/50**

Classic style

A most versatile classic mould and panel cutter with facility to reverse for scribing operations.

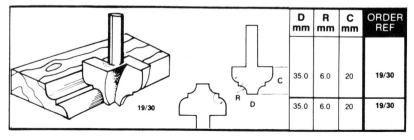

D mm	R mm	C mm	ORDER REF
35.0	6.0	20	**19/30**
35.0	6.0	20	**19/30**

Classic panel sets

The 20/2 and 20/3 offer attractive classic edge moulds, with matching scribing facility.

	D mm	R mm	C mm	ORDER REF
20/20 20/30	21.0	3.2	13.0	20/2
	25.0	3.2	12.0	20/20
				Set O(2)
	24.0	4.0	17.0	20/3
	28.5	4.0	14.2	20/30
				Set P(2)

Flat roman ogee

As with the classic mould cutter, the flat roman ogee fills a need in the furniture trades. It is ideal for profiling, e.g. cappings on decorative handrails, also raised and fielded panels.

D mm	C mm	R1 mm	R2 mm	ORDER REF
50 0	17 5	12 0	20 3	22/1

Dovetail/housing cutters

These are always preferred for strong joints in housings, drawers, and cupboards. The smallest cutter 31/10, is used as a 'key' for draught excluder strip. The largest in 32 group are used for stair housings.

C mm	D mm	A	ORDER REF
6.0	7	105°	31/10
9.0	10	100°	31/1
9.5	12	105°	31/2
14 0	14	100°	31/3
16 0	16	100°	31/5
17 0	18	100°	31/6
18.0	20	100°	31/7
24 5	14	95°	32/10
24 5	16	95°	32/1
25 5	19	95°	32/2
25 5	22	95°	32/3

Surfacing/edge strip

This 3 winged cutter is designed for:

a) Shallow surface cutting, smoothing and removing the groundings when relief carving.

b) Flushing hardwood edge strip.

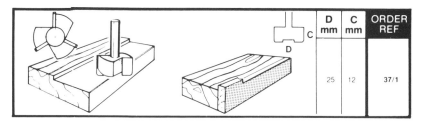

D mm	C mm	ORDER REF
25	12	37/1

Hinge sinkers

These tools are for use in both drilling machines and plunge routers. Their main function is to provide clean cut holes to receive circular hinges taps, and fittings. Best speed range 1,000–12,000 rpm.

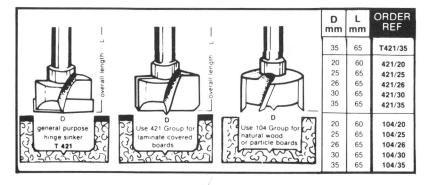

D mm	L mm	ORDER REF
35	65	T421/35
20	60	421/20
25	65	421/25
26	65	421/26
30	65	421/30
35	65	421/35
20	60	104/20
25	65	104/25
26	65	104/26
30	65	104/30
35	65	104/35

Drills/counter-sinks/counterbores and plug makers

For use in plunge routers and power drills. All have lip and spur solid carbide tips. Long life tools giving superb finish in most abrasive materials. Speed range 1,000–22,000 rpm.

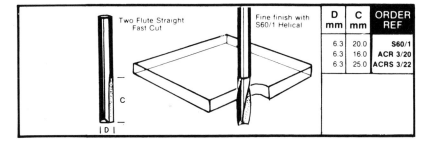

Wood Screw Size	D mm	C mm	E mm	ORDER REF
No. 8	3/16	20	—	61/80
No. 10	7/32	20	—	61/10
No. 12	1/4	20	—	61/12
				Set L (3)
No. 8	3/16	20	9.5	62/80
No. 10	7/32	20	12.0	62/10
No. 12	1/4	20	16.0	62/12
				Set H (3)
No. 8	3/16	20	9.5	63/80
No. 10	7/32	20	12	63/10
No. 12	1/4	20	16	63/12
				Set J (3)
No. 8	—	16	9.5	24/80
No. 10	—	16	12.0	24/10
No. 12	—	16	16.0	24/12
				Set K (3)

61 Group   62 Group   63 Group   24 Group

Acrylic cutters two flute – long life

For a superior finish, solid TC cutter S60/1 has helical fluting and is designed to cut and profile 'Perspex', 'Oroglas' and 'Plexiglas' and materials of similar consistency. Speeds 15,000–25,000 rpm.

	D mm	C mm	ORDER REF
	6.3	20.0	S60/1
	6.3	16.0	ACR 3/20
	6.3	25.0	ACRS 3/22

Two Flute Straight Fast Cut

Fine finish with S60/1 Helical

Aluminium cutters – two flute

This group of cutters is designed for grooving and milling non-ferrous metals. The 47/2 and 47/20 are recommended for surface cutting. Recommended speeds 10,000–25,000 rpm.

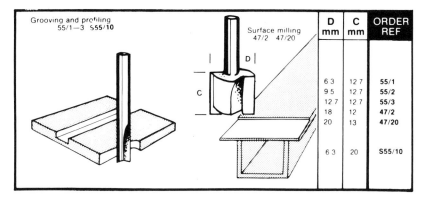

		D mm	C mm	ORDER REF
Grooving and profiling 55/1–3 S55/10	Surface milling 47/2 47/20			
		6 3	12 7	55/1
		9 5	12 7	55/2
		12 7	12 7	55/3
		18	12	47/2
		20	13	47/20
		6 3	20	S55/10

Fibre glass cutter – solid carbide

Mainly for cutting glass reinforced plastics, but suitable for shaping wood and deburring/grinding metal, using high speed hand motor (Rc. 10,000–30,000 rpm).

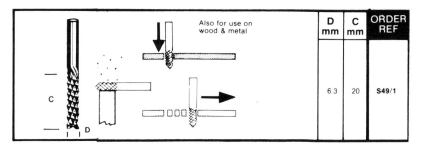

	D mm	C mm	ORDER REF
Also for use on wood & metal			
	6.3	20	S49/1

Shaped burrs – solid carbide

Ideal for grinding and deburring metal also for carving, shaping wood, and abrasive plastics. S49/5 is used also as a countersinker. Recommended speed ranges. For wood and plastics – 1,000 to 25,000 rpm. For metal – 10,000 to 40,000 rpm.

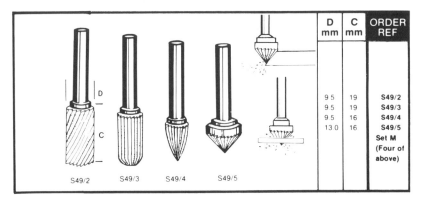

D mm	C mm	ORDER REF
9 5	19	S49/2
9 5	19	S49/3
9 5	16	S49/4
13 0	16	S49/5
		Set M
		(Four of above)

Aluminium/PVC cutters and countersinks

For standard drill and slot work choose 50 group, 55/08 for fine finish – recommended speeds 10,000–25,000 rpm. Countersink with 49/50 at 2,000–12,000 rpm. Drill/countersink 49/60 has a special stepped burr removal feature, recommended speed 2,000–5,000 rpm.

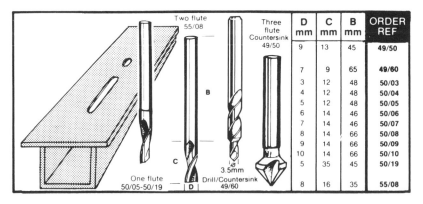

D mm	C mm	B mm	ORDER REF
9	13	45	49/50
7	9	65	49/60
3	12	48	50/03
4	12	48	50/04
5	12	48	50/05
6	14	46	50/06
7	14	46	50/07
8	14	66	50/08
9	14	66	50/09
10	14	66	50/10
5	35	45	50/19
8	16	35	55/08

Combination round over/ovolo sets

Two bearings are supplied as standard. With the 12.7mm (½in) Ø bearing, an ovolo mould is obtained; with a 16mm (⅝in) Ø bearing, a 'rounded over' shape is produced.

	C mm	R mm	D mm	B mm	ORDER REF
Cut with standard 12.7mm D Bearing	15.5	6.3	28		46/13
C	18.5	9.5	35	12.7 and	46/14
R B	21.0	12.7	41	16.0	46/15
	22	16	48		46/16
Cut with standard 16mm Bearing	Replacement bearing			12.7	B 127
	Replacement bearing			16.0	B 16

Roman ogee set

A Roman Ogee mould is obtained with a 12.7mm Ø bearing. Shallower mould effects are produced with other size bearings. (19mm Ø and 12.7mm Ø bearing supplied free.)

	C mm	R mm	D mm	B mm	ORDER REF
Cut with 12.7mm Bearing	12.7	4.0	28.5	12.7 and	46/23
Cut with alternative 16mm Bearing	19.0	6.3	38.2	19.0	46/24
Cut with standard 19mm	Replacement bearing			12.7	B 127
Bearing	Replacement bearing			19.0	B 19
	Alternative bearing			16	B 16

Classic decor set

This attractive classical mould cutter is now in demand for reproduction furniture and renovation of period joinery. Two bearings are supplied as standard 12.7mm and one 16mm Ø.

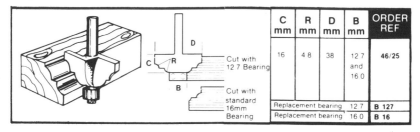

	C mm	R mm	D mm	B mm	ORDER REF
Cut with 12.7 Bearing	16	4.8	38	12.7 and 16.0	46/25
Cut with standard 16mm Bearing	Replacement bearing			12.7	B 127
	Replacement bearing			16.0	B 16

Cove mould sets

A Cove mould is obtained with the 12.7mm (½") Ø bearing fitted. Shallower radiused covers are produced with the 16mm and 19mm Ø bearings. (19mm Ø one is also supplied with set.)

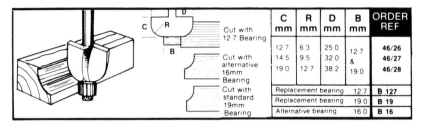

		C mm	R mm	D mm	B mm	ORDER REF
	Cut with 12.7 Bearing	12.7	6.3	25.0	12.7 & 19.0	46/26
	Cut with alternative 16mm Bearing	14.5	9.5	32.0		46/27
		19.0	12.7	38.2		46/28
	Cut with standard 19mm Bearing	Replacement bearing			12.7	B 127
		Replacement bearing			19.0	B 19
		Alternative bearing			16.0	B 16

Classic style sets

A new cutter to supplement the range of shapes required by those engaged in period furniture production. 12.7mm Ø and 16mm Ø bearing supplied with set.

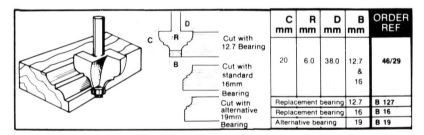

		C mm	R mm	D mm	B mm	ORDER REF
	Cut with 12.7 Bearing	20	6.0	38.0	12.7 & 16	46/29
	Cut with standard 16mm Bearing					
	Cut with alternative 19mm Bearing	Replacement bearing			12.7	B 127
		Replacement bearing			16	B 16
		Alternative bearing			19	B 19

Rabetting cutter set

Two bearings ½" Ø and 19mm Ø are supplied with this cutter to offer two rebate sizes. (A 16mm Ø one is an optional extra.)

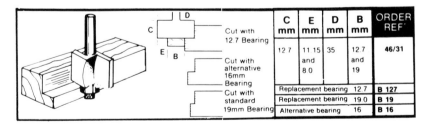

		C mm	E mm	D mm	B mm	ORDER REF
	Cut with 12.7 Bearing	12.7	11.15 and 8.0	35	12.7 and 19	46/31
	Cut with alternative 16mm Bearing					
	Cut with standard 19mm Bearing	Replacement bearing			12.7	B 127
		Replacement bearing			19.0	B 19
		Alternative bearing			16	B 16

Bead ovolo set

This new introduction offers several beads shapes by inter-changing or removing bearings. 12.7mm Ø and 16mm bearing supplied with set.

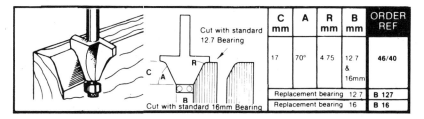

Cut with 12.7 Bearing	C mm	R mm	D mm	B mm	ORDER REF
		R1			
Cut with standard 16mm Bearing	16.2	6.4 R2 4.8	38	12.7 & 16	46/32
Cut with alternative 19mm Bearing	Replacement bearing			12.7	B 127
	Replacement bearing			16	B 16
	Alternative bearing			19	B 19

Rounding over/chamfer

This cutter was produced with skirtings and architraves in mind. It fills a need for 'on-site' machining work. The choice of two bearings, ½" Ø and 16mm Ø, gives added scope.

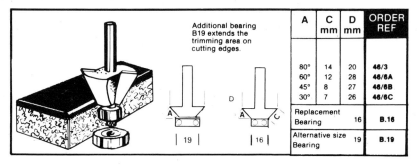

	C mm	A	R mm	B mm	ORDER REF
Cut with standard 12.7 Bearing	17	70°	4.75	12.7 & 16mm	46/40
	Replacement bearing	12.7			B 127
Cut with standard 16mm Bearing	Replacement bearing	16			B 16

Self guided trimmers (bevel). All TC

Similar to the type 46/2, these trimmers offer a choice of showing a wider edge line, with the laminate being trimmed at angles between 30 deg. and 80 deg.

Additional bearing B19 extends the trimming area on cutting edges.	A	C mm	D mm	ORDER REF
	80°	14	20	46/3
	60°	12	28	46/6A
	45°	8	27	46/6B
	30°	7	26	46/6C
	Replacement Bearing		16	B.16
	Alternative size Bearing		19	B.19

Double trim cutter. TC tipped

A time-saving cutter for trimming edges on top and bottom surfaces in one operation. The sleeved bearing follows the board between the two laminates.

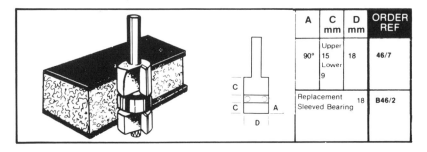

A	C mm	D mm	ORDER REF
90°	Upper 15 Lower 9	18	46/7
Replacement Sleeved Bearing		18	B46/2

Self guided trimmers 90°. All TC

Used mainly for trimming plastic laminates after bonding, but can be invaluable for copy profiling with roller bearing engaging on a template.

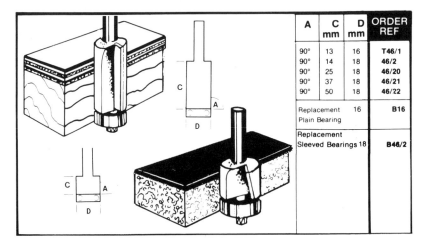

A	C mm	D mm	ORDER REF
90°	13	16	T46/1
90°	14	18	46/2
90°	25	18	46/20
90°	37	18	46/21
90°	50	18	46/22
Replacement Plain Bearing		16	B16
Replacement Sleeved Bearings		18	B46/2

Chamfer/raised panel cutters. All TC

When a chamfer effect is required and speed of operation is important, these cutters with inter-changeable bearings are invaluable. 12.7mm (½″) and 19mm Ø bearings are supplied standard.

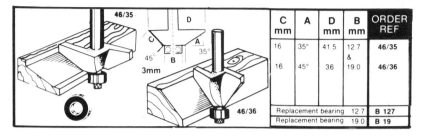

C mm	A	D mm	B mm	ORDER REF
16	35°	41.5	12.7	46/35
16	45°	36	& 19.0	46/36
Replacement bearing			12.7	B 127
Replacement bearing			19.0	B 19

Template/profile cutter

The ball-bearing follower is fitted above the cutter so that a pattern can be fitted on top of the workpiece. Can be used with router mounted above, or below table.

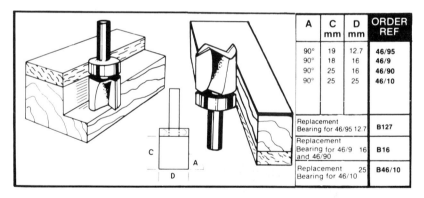

A	C mm	D mm	ORDER REF
90°	19	12.7	46/95
90°	18	16	46/9
90°	25	16	46/90
90°	25	25	46/10
Replacement Bearing for 46/95		12.7	B127
Replacement Bearing for 46/9 and 46/90		16	B16
Replacement Bearing for 46/10		25	B46/10

Staggered template cutters. All TC tipped

For cutting to a pattern in variance to the size of the template, cutters are offerd with bearings mounted on their shanks. Two securing flanges are supplied together with allen key to adjust them. (N.B. ¼" shanks only.)

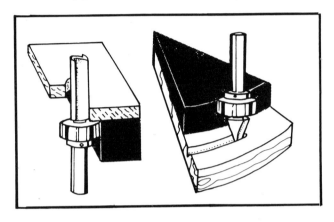

Trimmers for trimming top surface 90°. All TC

Designed for 90° trimming of laminated plastics. The 47/1 cutter accepts slotting blades. (See page 000 which describes range of SLA-H Slotters.)

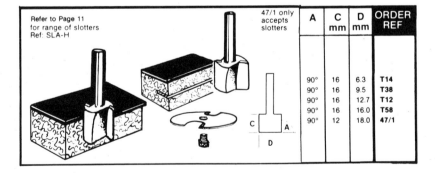

			A	C mm	D mm	ORDER REF
Refer to Page 11 for range of slotters Ref: SLA-H		47/1 only accepts slotters				
			90°	16	6.3	T14
			90°	16	9.5	T38
			90°	16	12.7	T12
			90°	16	16.0	T58
			90°	12	18.0	47/1

90° trimmers for trimming top and lipping. All TC

This cutter trims both vertical lipping (using the bottom cutting edge) and the overlapping horizontal edge. It is ideal for rebating all materials including aluminium.

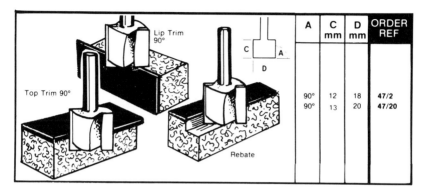

A	C mm	D mm	ORDER REF
90°	12	18	47/2
90°	13	20	47/20

Bevel trimmers for trimming top surface. All TC

An alternative to the 90° cutters for trimming laminates, when a wider edge line is preferred on the finished edge. Supplied in 80°, 60° and 30°.

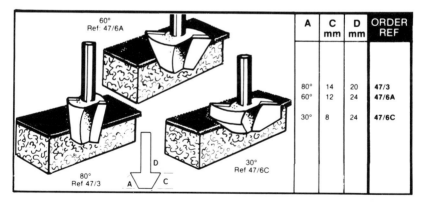

A	C mm	D mm	ORDER REF
80°	14	20	47/3
60°	12	24	47/6A
30°	8	24	47/6C

Combination trimmers for trimming top and lipping. TC tipped

Economical cutters, as they will perform three functions. They will trim the overlay at 90°, 45° or 60°, also the base of the cutter is used for trimming the vertical lipping.

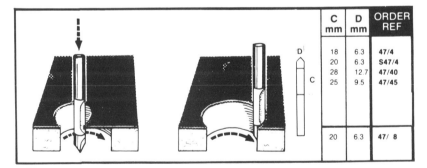

	A1	A2	C1 mm	C2 mm	D mm	ORDER REF
	45°	90°	10	6	21	**47/5**
	60°	90°	7	6	12	**47/7**

Pierce and trim cutters. All TC tipped

These cutters pierce and cut out apertures in laminate work tops. The base of the cutter acts as a guide follower.

C mm	D mm	ORDER REF
18	6.3	**47/4**
20	6.3	**S47/4**
28	12.7	**47/40**
25	9.5	**47/45**
20	6.3	**47/ 8**

'Economy' solid carbide trimmers

These 'economy' cutters are for the home craftsman on short runs of work. The S47/70 trims at 90° or 60° whilst the S48/40 is self guiding for 90° trimming.

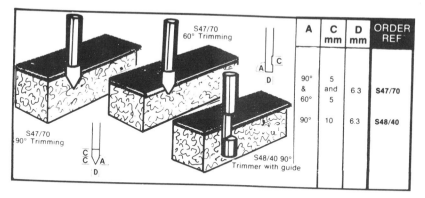

A	C mm	D mm	ORDER REF
90° & 60°	5 and 5	6 3	**S47/70**
90°	10	6 3	**S48/40**

Arbor sets – light and medium duty application

Ensure tools are mounted against the direction of motor spindle. *Refer to chart for suitable bearing selection.

DESCRIPTION		T mm	D mm	ORDER REF
Arbor without bearing				33/60
Arbor with B16 bearing				33/6
TCT Trimmer 1/4" bore	3 wing	10	16	34/6
TCT Slotters	2 wing	1.5	36	SL/A
and slitters	2 wing	2.0	36	SL/B
1/4" bore	2 wing	2.5	36	SL/C
	2 wing	3.0	36	SL/D
	2 wing	2.0	40	SL/E
	2 wing	2.5	50	SL/F
	2 wing	4.0	36	SL/G
	2 wing	5.5	36	SL/H
TCT Groovers	4 Wing	4.0	40	34/01
1/4" bore	4 Wing	6.0	40	34/20
	4 Wing	8.0	40	34/33
	3 Wing	10.0	40	34/41
Bearings		4.7	12.7	B127
1/4" bore		5.0	16.0	B16
		7.0	19.0	B19
		8.0	22.0	B22

Tongue & groove application

*This tongue and groover set, Ref. 336, fits all routers with a ⅜" Ø collet and rated at minimum 1,000 watts.

*It comprises of one 33/60 arbor, one 6mm Kerf TC groover, 34/20, and one 10mm Kerf groover 34/41.

*Not to be used on ¼" or 8mm shank arbors.

DESCRIPTION		T mm	D mm	ORDER REF
TCT Tongue and Groover Set Comprising all three below.				336
Arbor without bearing				33/60
TCT Groovers	4 wing	6.0	40	34/20
	3 wing	10.0	40	34/41

Typical 20mm Finish T & G Board

Making the tongue

Making the groove

Arbor sets
Heavy duty applications – undercutting
*The flush cutting base of the undercut groover, is much in demand for weather strip insertion.
*It threads onto arbor so as to give a flush base.
*The 33/20 arbor allows for a self-guide bearing so as to dispense with a side fence

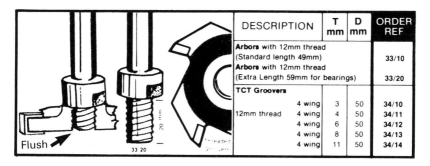

DESCRIPTION		T mm	D mm	ORDER REF
Arbors with 12mm thread (Standard length 49mm)				33/10
Arbors with 12mm thread (Extra Length 59mm for bearings)				33/20
TCT Groovers				
	4 wing	3	50	**34/10**
12mm thread	4 wing	4	50	**34/11**
	4 wing	6	50	**34/12**
	4 wing	8	50	**34/13**
	4 wing	11	50	**34/14**

Heavy duty application – long arbor type
*These long heavy duty arbors are chosen for fitting the larger groovers and blades.
*Controlled cutting depths are obtained from selected guide bearings.

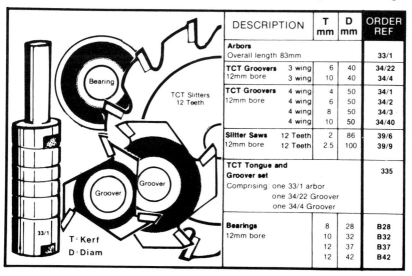

DESCRIPTION		T mm	D mm	ORDER REF
Arbors Overall length 83mm				33/1
TCT Groovers 12mm bore	3 wing	6	40	**34/22**
	3 wing	10	40	**34/4**
TCT Groovers 12mm bore	4 wing	4	50	**34/1**
	4 wing	6	50	**34/2**
	4 wing	8	50	**34/3**
	4 wing	10	50	**34/40**
Slitter Saws 12mm bore	12 Teeth	2	86	**39/6**
	12 Teeth	2.5	100	**39/9**
TCT Tongue and Groover set Comprising: one 33/1 arbor one 34/22 Groover one 34/4 Groover				335
Bearings 12mm bore		8	28	**B28**
		10	32	**B32**
		12	37	**B37**
		12	42	**B42**

T = Kerf
D = Diam

Classic profile scriber set – PR-SC/4

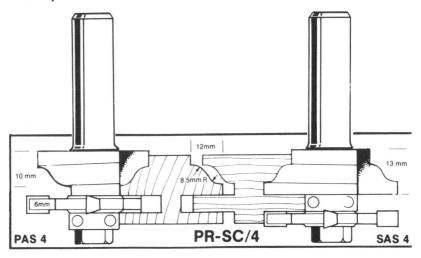

Classic profile scriber set – PR-SC/5

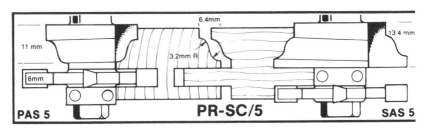

Classic profile scriber set – PR-SC/6

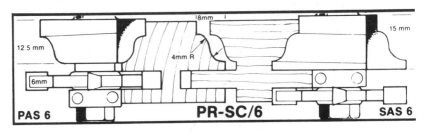

Classic profile scriber set PR-SC/7

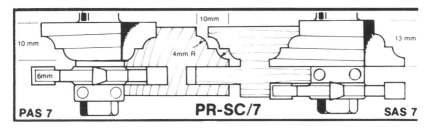

Ovolo profile/scriber set PR-SC/8

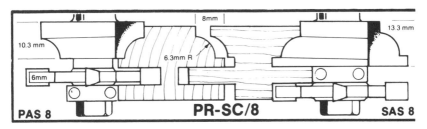

Ovolo/round profile/scriber set PR-SC/9

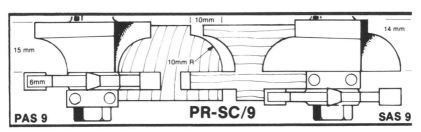

Raised panel profile/scriber set PR-SC/10

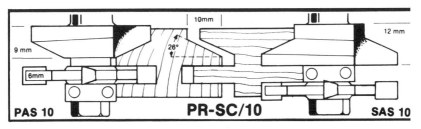

Cutting depth chart

How to use it. When a special cutting depth is needed for a slotter, slitter or groover, subtract the bearing diameter from tool diameter and divide by two. Chart below will tell you which bearing to select.

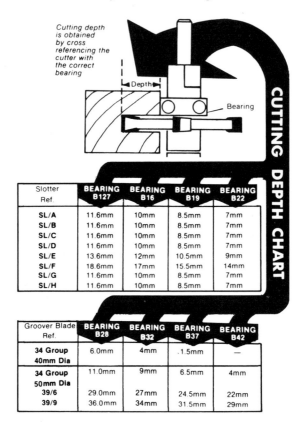

Slotter Ref.	BEARING B127	BEARING B16	BEARING B19	BEARING B22
SL/A	11.6mm	10mm	8.5mm	7mm
SL/B	11.6mm	10mm	8.5mm	7mm
SL/C	11.6mm	10mm	8.5mm	7mm
SL/D	11.6mm	10mm	8.5mm	7mm
SL/E	13.6mm	12mm	10.5mm	9mm
SL/F	18.6mm	17mm	15.5mm	14mm
SL/G	11.6mm	10mm	8.5mm	7mm
SL/H	11.6mm	10mm	8.5mm	7mm

Groover Blade Ref.	BEARING B28	BEARING B32	BEARING B37	BEARING B42
34 Group 40mm Dia	6.0mm	4mm	.1.5mm	—
34 Group 50mm Dia	11.0mm	9mm	6.5mm	4mm
39/6	29.0mm	27mm	24.5mm	22mm
39/9	36.0mm	34mm	31.5mm	29mm

New cutter shapes – half actual size. All TCT

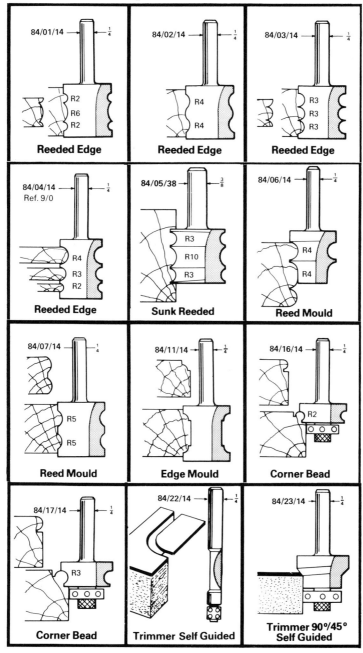

84/01/14 ¼	84/02/14 ¼	84/03/14 ¼
R2 R6 R2	R4 R4	R3 R3 R3
Reeded Edge	**Reeded Edge**	**Reeded Edge**
84/04/14 ¼ Ref. 9/0	84/05/38 ⅜	84/06/14 ¼
R4 R3 R2	R3 R10 R3	R4 R4
Reeded Edge	**Sunk Reeded**	**Reed Mould**
84/07/14 ¼	84/11/14 ¼	84/16/14 ¼
R5 R5		R2
Reed Mould	**Edge Mould**	**Corner Bead**
84/17/14 ¼	84/22/14 ¼	84/23/14 ¼
R3		
Corner Bead	**Trimmer Self Guided**	**Trimmer 90°/45° Self Guided**

New cutter shapes – half actual size. All TCT

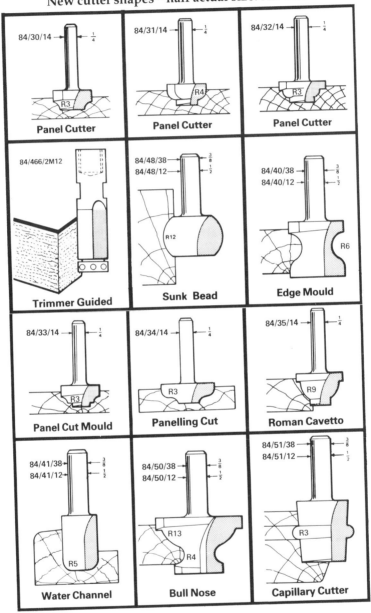

84/30/14 → ← $\frac{1}{4}$

Panel Cutter

84/31/14 → ← $\frac{1}{4}$

R4

Panel Cutter

84/32/14 → ← $\frac{1}{4}$

R3

Panel Cutter

84/466/2M12

Trimmer Guided

84/48/38 → $\frac{3}{8}$
84/48/12 → $\frac{1}{2}$

R12

Sunk Bead

84/40/38 → $\frac{3}{8}$
84/40/12 → $\frac{1}{2}$

R6

Edge Mould

84/33/14 → ← $\frac{1}{4}$

R3

Panel Cut Mould

84/34/14 → ← $\frac{1}{4}$

R3

Panelling Cut

84/35/14 → ← $\frac{1}{4}$

R9

Roman Cavetto

84/41/38 → $\frac{3}{8}$
84/41/12 → $\frac{1}{2}$

R5

Water Channel

84/50/38 → $\frac{3}{8}$
84/50/12 → $\frac{1}{2}$

R13
R4

Bull Nose

84/51/38 → $\frac{3}{8}$
84/51/12 → $\frac{1}{2}$

R3

Capillary Cutter

New cutter shapes – half actual size. All TCT

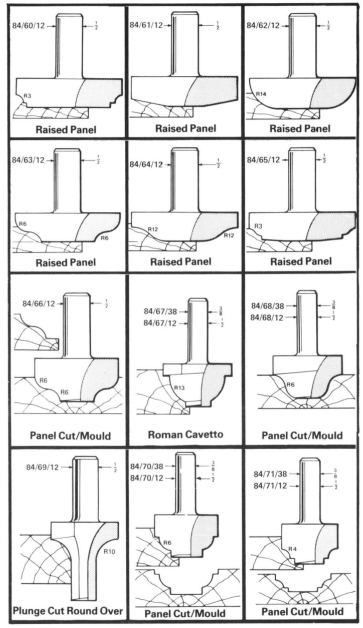

84/60/12 $\frac{1}{2}$	84/61/12 $\frac{1}{2}$	84/62/12 $\frac{1}{2}$
R3		R14
Raised Panel	**Raised Panel**	**Raised Panel**

84/63/12 $\frac{1}{2}$	84/64/12 $\frac{1}{2}$	84/65/12 $\frac{1}{2}$
R6 R6	R12 R12	R3
Raised Panel	**Raised Panel**	**Raised Panel**

84/66/12 $\frac{1}{2}$	84/67/38 $\frac{3}{8}$ 84/67/12 $\frac{1}{2}$	84/68/38 $\frac{3}{8}$ 84/68/12 $\frac{1}{2}$
R6 R6	R13	R6
Panel Cut/Mould	**Roman Cavetto**	**Panel Cut/Mould**

84/69/12 $\frac{1}{2}$	84/70/38 $\frac{3}{8}$ 84/70/12 $\frac{1}{2}$	84/71/38 $\frac{3}{8}$ 84/71/12 $\frac{1}{2}$
R10	R6	R4
Plunge Cut Round Over	**Panel Cut/Mould**	**Panel Cut/Mould**

18 Appendix

Design your own shapes

Readers who can might feel overwhelmed by the huge range of cutters described on previous pages, might feel relieved to know there are simple means of compounding standard shapes. Indeed, from a mere half dozen router bits, non-standard shapes can be obtained with comparative ease.

Nowadays moulded edged and shaped work are tending to replace the rather harsh lines seen on some modern furniture and the field is open for the individual imagination to fulfil itself. If an ovolo or simple round shape is required on a moulding then the choice of cutters presents no problem and the correct one can be selected, but if you have a preference for a non-standard shape what then? To produce a special cutter to suit the need would cost in the region of £50 and such expense is hardly justified to satisfy a creative whim. There is a solution not based on a big bank balance, but a little imagination and shape solution system offered by the Trend cutter advisory service.

The "Identicut System" is a method of choosing the right cutter or cutters to produce a non-standard shape. It works like this: the envisaged end section of the moulding is drawn up and various cutter shapes are superimposed on the drawing to give an immediate visual reference without having to work with the cutters themselves. Alternatively the shapes can be marked out on tracing paper and placed on the drawing for the same effect.

Using this system it is possible to visualise immediately how a series of standard cutters can produce a non-standard shape. Figs 72 show a selection of shapes that can be obtained by the

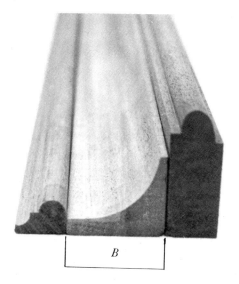

B

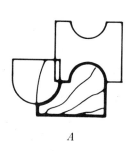

A

C

Fig.72. The compound mould shape illustrated was built-up from three separate sections. (A) This mould was created by first running a staff bead type 9, followed by a radiused cutter type 12. (B) This cove mould was the product of a spindle moulder. (25mm radius being too large for the router). (C) This mould was obtained from a staff bead type cutter ref. 9/20. This compound of moulds was used for central part of a grandfather clock detailed in a previous chapter.

Fig.72.1. Examples of non-standard shapes, produced by standard cutters readily available.

method described. Obviously, there are dozens of other profiles that a fertile imagination can bring forth, because shape configurations are unlimited.

This system could be particularly useful when trying to match up architraves and skirting boards in old properties and could well be used to convert existing standard mouldings to the shape required.

The grand looking mould seen in Fig. 72, was worked out by craftsman Ralph Fellows, for his grandfather clock. The left hand mould A was performed with cove cutter 12/7, and the halfround top with staff bead ref. 9/1. The centre large cove radius B came from his spindle moulder. The right hand top mould C was machined with profile cutter ref. 9/20.

If in doubt, work out your ideas and make a dummy run on scrap timber before committing yourself to the real thing. Individuality in woodworking can easily be achieved if sufficient thought and imagination is applied to every day tools. The router is the prime example of a creative power tool, and its potential is literally unlimited.

Information about sources of supply for equipment mentioned in this book, is available from: TREND MACHINERY AND CUTTING TOOLS LTD. UNIT N, PENFOLD WORKS, IMPERIAL WAY, WATFORD, HERTS, ENGLAND, WD2 4YY TEL. 0923-49911/55699

19 Metric/imperial conversional chart

For the benefit of our friends in the 'new world', where metric sizes are not commonly used, we give a conversion chart to show size comparisons between millimetres and fractions of an inch.

CONVERSION

INCHES	64th	MM
		0·5 / 1
1/32	1/64	0·5
	3/64	1
1/16		1·5
	5/64	2
3/32	7/64	2·5
1/8		3
		3·5
5/32	9/64	4
	11/64	4·5
3/16	13/64	5
7/32	15/64	5·5
		6
1/4	17/64	6·5
		7
9/32	19/64	7·5
	21/64	8
5/16		8·5
11/32	23/64	9
		9·5
3/8	25/64	10
13/32	27/64	10·5
	29/64	11
7/16		11·5
15/32	31/64	12
		12·5
1/2	33/64	13
17/32	35/64	13·5
9/16		14
	37/64	14·5
19/32	39/64	15
		15·5
5/8	41/64	16
21/32	43/64	16·5
11/16		17
	45/64	17·5
23/32	47/64	18
		18·5
3/4		19

INCHES	64th	MM
3/4		19
	49/64	19·5
25/32	51/64	20
13/16		20·5
	53/64	21
27/32	55/64	21·5
		22
7/8	57/64	22·5
29/32	59/64	23
		23·5
15/16	61/64	24
31/32	63/64	24·5
		25
1		25·5
1/32	1/64	26
		26·5
1/16	3/64	27
	5/64	27·5
3/32	7/64	28
		28·5
1/8	9/64	29
5/32	11/64	29·5
3/16	13/64	30
		30·5
7/32	15/64	31
		31·5
1 1/4	17/64	32
9/32	19/64	32·5
5/16		33
	21/64	33·5
11/32	23/64	34
		34·5
3/8	25/64	35
13/32	27/64	35·5
7/16		36
	29/64	36·5
15/32	31/64	37
		37·5
1 1/2		38

INDEX